Trust Your Intuition

A Guide to Living Your Authentic Life

Robin Pollak

Trust Your Intuition: A Guide to Living Your Authentic Life

Paperback ISBN: 9781958714096
Ebook ISBN: 9781958714102
Library of Congress Control Number: 2022942602

CHICAGO · NEW YORK · PARIS · ROME

Muse Literary
3319 N. Cicero Avenue
Chicago IL 60641-9998

This book was written from my perspective. The memories that I am sharing (that include family and friends) may, in your mind, be reflected differently; but, this is what I saw, felt and experienced.

Dedication

i.l.y. 4784

JDP^2

For Cooper, Maggie, Chelsea,
Jade, Jeri, Dezi, Luci, and Rhoda

Contents

INTRODUCTION

I am always curious about how to look at things with a new lens. A new perspective has allowed me to see things within myself. The more I learned about my connection to my intuitive side the more I was able to trust myself in all things. In many ways the process of writing is "the dance of not doing." I was able to give myself the permission to allow things to marinate in my mind. To get curious. In so many ways this book is a representation of me saying yes to myself. There were so many times that I stopped and started this book. Writing this book has given me a chance to expand my intuitive skills. I recognized that my ability to channel and receive information from my guides was in fact further acceptance of my gifts. Each time I was at a crossroads about continuing to write. I would say yes to myself and continue. In doing that I was affirming and acknowledging all the steps I have taken over these past four years.

Something you should know is that all the titles are in fact channeled messages. This book is for all of you who are intuitive or curious. The personal stories that I share are a guide to accompany you on your journey.

Each title is a channeled message that I further expanded on in the essay.

Channels will appear in italics.

The book is written so you can read it the way it is laid out or you can go to the index and read the essay based on the information you are seeking that day. You may find yourself reading the whole book out of sequence. That's perfect. There is a meditation after each essay, which allows you to sink further into the energy of the essay.

My hope is that you can find yourself in the stories that I wrote. And I wish for you that this information is the catalyst for you to become even more curious than you were before.

It is my intention that you take from these stories what resonates with you and let go of what doesn't serve you.

I didn't have a plan or a specific process other than trusting that I needed to continue to share my experience and wisdom. Along the way I have learned more about myself. My wish is that you can uncover more of yourself. Give yourself permission to explore. I have learned through this work how important it is to give myself permission to be. "Daydreaming for Warriors" is the original idea of what eventually became this book. It represents the dance of not doing. It is the permission to be. Too many times I caught myself in a twirl where my mind would spin, thinking about what I "should" be doing or how things should be done. My wish is that the stories in this book allow you to give yourself the gift of having permission to do it your way.

So that you could begin to fully embrace yourself authenticity with love and compassion.

1

Tap Into Your Wisdom

Are you familiar with the "shoulda coulda" dance? It is a dance I have done for many years, and I am here to tell you it is a waste of time. Things happen when they are meant to. I would inwardly roll my eyes when people said, "Don't do the shoulda woulda coulda dance" in an effort to cheer me up. The thing is, there is a reason we have resistance. For me, it was fear of change, judgment, and difficulty trusting myself, just to name a few. I had this notion that I knew things that I couldn't explain. I would hear voices. I just didn't completely trust that the information I heard was real. I also had no idea how to connect to the voices or even if I should. I could accept the notion that people were psychic. I was fascinated with the notion. I was drawn to it. I was not skeptical, however; I am a New Yorker and knew people could be scammers. So, I didn't trust just any psychic to help me understand what was happening. I questioned myself all the time, wondering if it was my imagination.

My intuition was something that I wore like someone who puts on a forgotten sweater in the bottom of your drawer. You know, the one that gets buried because it doesn't make the cut to enter into the favorites category. So, when I would find it scrunched up in a ball and I would shake it out and put it on, it felt itchy and confining and within minutes I would take it off and stash it back. I felt like I didn't know how to claim my psychic gifts or even if it was something to claim. It is like when I get a new gadget and attempt to use it without reading the directions. You know what I mean—it felt strange and unfamiliar. It took me a long time to recognize I had an intuition that I could lean on when I needed to access more wisdom. I was great in a crisis operating on pure instinct. However, deciding when to rely on it in less emergent scenarios seemed daunting. When I began to understand that everyone has intuition, I realized that so many of us are denying our inner wisdom. I started to think about this and thought, *what are the ingredients I need to begin to trust mine?* I considered this and thought of the ingredients like one would think when they were making soup. I puttered around as I do when I am trying to figure something out. I knew that I had to develop trust, faith, love, and compassion in myself. I wanted to stop second-guessing what I thought. When I began to do this, it felt uncomfortable, like I was wearing someone else's shoes. It is because I was. I was putting on the shoes of a person who believed in themselves and knew that they had worth and value.

Do you have a pair of slippers that you love? I do and one day I looked down at my slippers with the coffee stains and some other stain I could not identify and decided I needed a new pair. So I bought a new pair, and when they came, I stuffed them in the back of the bottom of my closet. Have you done this? Thinking I will wear them soon. As if wearing these new slippers would mean I was letting go of my comfort. I guess figuratively I am. It takes a while to trust the new slippers will provide comfort and respite you need when you need support. Then one day I decided to just dig them out and wear them. I just grabbed the same ones the next day. I looked down at my feet as I slipped on the left slipper and noticed my old trusty pair on the floor of my closet and my heart squeezed a little. Like I was discarding a piece of me. I smiled and realized that I outgrew those old slippers in so many ways. It was time for me to trust something new. That these new slippers made me feel good and would be as good if not even better. I needed to allow myself to take a leap of trust and believe. I left on my new slippers, but it took me a while before I could toss the old ones. Pretty soon I forgot I had them. Then one day I was putting on my earring in my closet and I dropped it. I dropped to my hand and knees and looked amongst the shoes on the floor in my closet and the occasional dust bunny for the earring. There in the back next to my earring were my old slippers. I looked at them and chuckled. It was time to throw them out. I had moved on and my new slippers were feeling lived in and perfect. I needed to give myself a chance to let the new ideas I was learning about myself to take root. I needed to remember that all this inner work is itself a process. I need to always remember to show compassion to myself for all that I am.

This is a process that I was committed to. Personal growth I have discovered, is not a destination with a finite goal. It is a choice to be willing to do the inner work I need. Once I learned to let go of things in my life that just weren't working. I could create the space to believe in who I was.

I can see that denying my worth and trust in myself allowed me to let go of the most precious part of me. I was lost, always looking to everyone outside of myself for their approval.

Gaging my behavior based on everyone I respected instead of my own. I allowed myself to become very small. I really believe that if we lose our connection to our intuition then we lose the essence of who we are. This book is about how I started to accept my intuition. The choice is within you to tap into yours.

Something to Consider

The truth is we all have intuition, and we deny it. When we question the trust in ourselves, we are saying we are not enough. Instead, we need to nurture the part that allows us to have trust and faith and recognize our value and worth. When we deny our intuition, we are letting go of the most precious piece of us. We are lost. In an effort to turn off the flow to your intuition, you also turn off the most intrinsic part of you. Intuition is the guiding light. (We stop listening to our inner wisdom when making decisions, when making connections, and when fulfilling our dreams.) We risk losing the essence of who we are. This book is about how I started to accept my intuition. The choice is within you to tap into yours.

There was a time when I felt the desire to be more connected to myself. I could feel this yearning within. I believe it was a sign I needed to allow new information in. To be open to experiencing new ideas to deepen my connection to who I was. It was this sudden shift of an awakening within me. I began to look at things in a new light. Shifting old patterns and thoughts and expanding an inner evolution.

To begin this practice, you need to give yourself permission to daydream or "putter." The ability to allow thoughts to come into your mind without judgment. To gift yourself the time to not pressure yourself to think or do. It sounds strange but I believe this space is where the magic starts to be discovered. The freedom to actually allow yourself the time to wonder. In all the ideas you start to unravel what is important to you. Start writing these ideas down. It is also important to indulge in this activity every day for ten minutes or more. I used to think that how much work I produced was important, but I quickly learned it had to be connected to what I believed so that what I was doing was driven by passion.

Surround yourself with people who are willing to shift their thinking patterns. Be prepared to shift old belief patterns that are holding you in a story where your dreams feel unattainable. When we begin to unravel our old beliefs, we allow space to consider new ideas and trust our dreams. We begin to seed our ideas and then take steps to move from mere thinking to the creation of what our ideas could bring to the world. That is how we discover our passion. That passion is the energy that drives us to a deeper connection to what we believe. Once we believe that, we begin to trust in our worth and value and step into a new version of who we are. Our ego will come out and cause us to question our choices. The version of us who did not connect to our soul seems so distant. We now know to trust the daydreamer within us and let her light shine.

CHANNEL

In your most quiet moments
You discovered
who you are
that part of you
That doesn't
need permission
to come out
be seen
Be heard
Be acknowledged

The permission
Needs to come from within
You need to see all your gifts
claim them as yours
Glory in all you are
Create a timeline
In the future
Where your light can shine
You can stand in the worth
of who you are
Know your wisdom
Omaya

AFFIRMATION

I can acknowledge my gift

INSPIRATION

A space to discover your gift

2

There is a stillness that must happen within us before we can grow

When we notice that we feel off-balance or even sick, it is our body's way to release old information, old stories, and make room for new integration because there is an upgrade coming.

I've always been intrigued with anything in the genre of personal growth. I felt if I understood myself in greater depth, I could live a more authentic life.

The problem was I was always listening to and looking at situations outside of myself. When I began this journey to understand my intuitive gifts, I quickly realized that what I needed to do was look within. I'd spent too long judging my actions based on how I measured up to other people's beliefs about me. Before I could look inside, I needed to have trust and faith in what I'd find. That is where the true work is. I needed to let go of the idea that everyone else held the answers for me. I had this unconscious desire to stop the victim triangle I was living in. I spent too long being the victim, blaming who I believed was the abuser and then seeking a rescuer. By choosing daily to commit to connecting to my higher self and intuition, I began to believe in *myself* and explore the idea that the information and wisdom I received was something I could believe and trust. Stepping into the shoes of being my own rescuer.

It is not about being right. It was about the belief that I contained value. I was worthy. These two ideas took me a long while to wrap my head around. I knew when I contributed to the world, I had worth;

however, the idea that I had value and worth just being me without doing anything for someone else was hard to embrace. Looking back, I now realize that believing I have value and worth by simply being me was and is my most important lesson. When I work with clients, I facilitate their ability to see their own worth. I know now how invaluable this knowledge is, but for many years it escaped me.

I remember the first time I was on a call with my coach, and she asked me, "Do you love yourself?" After I rolled my eyes, I hesitated in answering and took a breath. If you know me at all, that is not me. I stumbled around feeling like I had to fill the empty space with something, then I spit out, "I love that I am compassionate and patient." I could read the energy in the pause that followed my answer that she was looking for a different response. At that time that was all I could offer. This question sent all the alarm buzzers off in my head. The truth was I liked who I was but love myself? Isn't that something you get from someone else?

Learning to have greater compassion for myself and learning how to release judgment about all the zingers or triggers that come my way that propel me to question my value and worth. Those triggers had me questioning if I was enough. The never-ending conversation I would have in my head when I wondered if I should have done it differently. That is when I have a conversation with myself and say, "Hey, you, stop doing the 'shoulda, woulda' dance!" It is easy for me to take a step down the familiar road of feeling frustrated and defensive. It is a space I go to when I let my ego take the driver's seat. What typically happens is once all that energy burns out, I typically problem-solve and figure out what to do next by allowing my intuition to lead the way. I never used to take the time to ask myself. I never had compassion or trust in myself. I took the criticisms and licked my wounds, but I rarely looked at the situation and thought about how I showed up. I was always looking at the outcome. Before I fully trusted in myself, I was easily overwhelmed and felt very anxious whenever I had to make decisions. I was so used to making decisions based on what a group of people thought, not what I knew. This left me feeling unsure and easily overwhelmed and agitated. I was impatient, frustrated, and highly critical of myself. I began to notice I even disliked creating big goals. What if I failed? The love language I was operating was based on how I was viewed by others.

SOMETHING TO CONSIDER

We think in order to change we need to identify the problem and set about fixing it. What if there was nothing to fix? What if the things we believe to be problems or negative traits are really gifts? When we start to hold more compassion for who we are in the now moment, we begin to let go of the need to please everyone. Close your eyes for a moment and remember a time when you experienced love. It could be the love of a person, a pet, or even an experience. Remember how you felt. How did this love feel in your body? Now think of expanding your heart to feel this love for you. Creating that connection to memories lets you see that you can hold love on your own and anchor into it always. When we can receive love, we can attract love in our lives.

CHANNEL

Create the vision of how you love
[It] can touch the souls you reach
The energy to reach them
is not yours to manage or claim

It is their journey
to create the space
to discover their value
Waiting for the pinnacle moment
when they can see the value of who they are
The time to claim
to celebrate who they desire to be.

You can create
The space
it is theirs to step into
Create a space
for them to witness their greatness
To unfold
what lies underneath
To release the joy
Release the fear
Release the judgment
To walk the steps
you have walked
to discover their innate authenticity

AFFIRMATION

I am worthy

INSPIRATION

Find your voice

3

Permission Comes from Within

Death is a topic that is difficult to discuss and there is no right or wrong way to grieve. There is no protocol. There is so much fear surrounding death. It is a conversation many people have in their own minds. I avoided sharing until I was asked directly because of the way people reacted when I shared that my mother died when I was three. There were times when I would be at a friend's house after school. So excited to have a playdate. I remember this one particular playdate when I was seven, and we were sitting around the kitchen table, having tuna and Ritz crackers. My friend's mom sat down with us with her coffee and started asking me questions about the age span between me and my sister and my sister and my brother. I just explained between bites of tuna and sips of Tang. All the details. I didn't think about why she wanted to know at the time. She began to cry and reached out to embrace me, which felt suffocating and awkward. I quickly learned to share as little as possible, even if asked, because once people found out the real story, there was this awkward tension in the air. They were sad and just never knew what to say to me. I never knew what to say; it was just a fact. I never realized that they were holding space for my grief. The thing is I never felt I deserved the compassion. I never grieved. My father and my sister grieved, not me. I didn't realize until much later that I didn't know how to accept the sympathy since I always thought it wasn't my loss. I protect myself from the pain of the loss. Being in a place to receive sympathy meant I needed to allow myself to begin to feel worthy of healing.

When I was in my thirties, I decided to see a therapist to teach me how to do self-hypnosis. I had this idea that if I could be under hypnosis, I could piece together memories I shared with my mother. The hypnosis was interesting, but it did not allow me to gain a deeper connection or acquire lost memories. Then, through conversations with my therapist, I came to understand that I held a great deal of judgment about my inability to connect to Mom at her grave. I tried to go to mediums and connect, but they couldn't connect to my mom. My therapist and I explored this on a deeper level, and I came to have compassion for little me and understand how I couldn't judge little me for not holding on to those memories. I understood this because I wouldn't expect my children to do this. Somehow that idea created such sadness in my heart. How much love I shared with my children, and if I died, I too would not be remembered. These thoughts brought up so much grief about how hard it must have been for my mom at thirty-six to know that I would forget her. In that space I felt this deep connection and began to get in touch with my own grief.

The grief rode in like a freight train. No one except my husband Kevin knew I was grieving for my mother for the first time in thirty-five years. I shared my pain with no one and went about my life as if it was a typical day. I realized I needed support. The truth was I was experiencing her loss as if it had just happened. I started sharing it with people close to me and even mentioned it to my sister. I held so much anger toward her that she had her for twelve years and all those memories were locked within her. I somehow understood how those were hers. The last pieces of our mom she would have. My dad was a whole other story. I felt so torn about how I could go on each day and keep all the information compartmentalized and stamped it private. I never really allowed myself to get angry at him. I always swallowed down whatever I was feeling. I felt so isolated; this was a shared memory, and yet somehow, because of my age, I had no memory. I somehow understood why they held onto them so tight. On another level I was confused and frustrated that I was not in on the information that I was part of. I felt isolated and not part of the family. Feeling left out has been a trigger for me for a long time. I never understood it. It took me a long time to come to a place where I accepted what they could give, and I basically stopped asking. I was in a new place of understanding about my loss, and I was able to share my story with people and when they shared their condolences, I was able to receive them. I knew that my mother's loss did not belong only to my sister and my dad. It belonged to me.

When I was five, I was in my room playing with my dolls, and my dad knocked on the door. He was wearing a plaid shirt that was short-sleeved and a pair of khaki trousers. He always had this clean smell that I loved, and the smell drifted into the room before he even opened the door. The door creaked open. I knew it was him without even looking. He was carrying a manila envelope and a frame. He asked me to come over to him. He handed me this big envelope but held onto the frame. He told me he wanted me to have these pictures of my mother but to keep them in my drawer, so I didn't upset Gerda (my stepmother). We opened up my top drawer and he placed the frame face down and the big yellow envelope on top of it. He put my clothes back on top and closed the drawer. He waited for me to close the drawer, making sure it was hidden from sight. My dad sent me a small smile and closed the door. I didn't even question him. I sensed this was important to him. After he left, I opened the drawer and dug out the frame. I looked at my mom in the photo and touched her smile through the glass frame. At that moment I knew that conversations about my mother were off-limits. I didn't understand it, but it wasn't until much later that I questioned it. I knew where they were. I had a piece of my mom inside my dresser. I kept them there safe in my underwear drawer so I could see her face every day. I didn't take them out of the drawer until I moved out of my parents' house. It was time for these pictures of us to be seen. I put them on a dresser at first, and eventually, I put them in my family room on a shelf. It wasn't until I had my son that I received a message from her. They are precious to me. Below is one I received recently.

CHANNEL

It was bestowed upon your soul
When you were created
your wisdom and light are a gift
Bestowed by angels and guides
Who saw your light
In another life
Another time
Waiting
For you to see

See it in your own eyes
Stop Waiting to see it [in] another
I believe you are looking for my love in all the eyes you see
I am here
My love is endless
You feel it
Know how to recognize it in you
Be strong my beautiful girl
Be brave
Be light
Be curious
My love surrounds you always

A MESSAGE FOR YOU

When we are in pain we need all our resources to make it through. My Aunt Rose told me that sometimes when you are in an emergency you need to take things five minutes at a time and if that's too much you take it a moment at n time. When I think about how my brother and sister grieved our parents loss, we all did it in our own way. The greatest gift we can give ourselves is the ability to not judge ourselves for what your soul needs; instead, gift yourself with time to heal. I was lucky to have my brother and sister because they showed up when I could not.

The energy you gift yourself to honor your feelings will be what is needed as you allow time to move forward past this moment.

CHANNEL

Tears allow us to release and heal.
Time is now to allow love to come to you
To be able to receive and be held up by the those who can
gift you with the space to be
Allow the time to be of one that grants you the permission to
Be still
To cry
To be alone
To laugh
To remember

AFFIRMATION

I give myself permission

INSPIRATION

Within each of us

4

ALONE YOU FIND IT DEEP WITHIN

When I started this whole spiritual journey, I had a very systematic ritual that I followed every day. I woke up each day and I chose to be in a place of openness and possibility of what the universe could deliver and bring. I didn't have a specific expectation. I was open to seeing what would come. Then one day after weeks of doing this ritual I found that I was feeling a lack of connection. I was worried that I had somehow lost this gift. When I spoke to my mentor, she told me that I didn't need the ritual anymore. I had what I needed inside of me. I could access it wherever and whenever I wanted. I was surprised and tried it out. I found that I knew what that feeling was when I connected. I could sense it in the center of my heart. I knew what it felt like in my mind. It wasn't that I had lost anything; it was all about a new perspective of what I'd gained. Creating stillness for me is allowing myself the time to go inside myself and connect to something greater than myself. It requires me to have faith and trust that what I'm feeling is real and to believe what I feel and what I know. Without taking the time to create stillness in my life, I would've never discovered this.

My new way of creating stillness is *puttering*—the little things that I do in my house allow my mind to wander and think without forcefully making myself think of anything in particular. All the lists, all the planning charts, and things that a lot of people do to organize themselves simply don't work for me. This is not to say that I don't use lists and I don't use charts, but when I'm in a creative mode and I'm trying to tap into my intuition, those methods don't serve me. Each of us needs to figure out what works for us and how to find that space to identify our intuition and listen to what it is saying. Each time I am in a course, or I am listening to a podcast on personal development I always hear the suggestion to create a ritual. As soon as I hear it, that's my cue to do what works for me. I trust in myself to know what works for me. I am resistant to any ritual; I thrive in open spaces. Creating moments where I can let my mind wander. I have tried countless times to have hard routines. I work better with looser constraints. I just accept this and know intuitively that I have times in my day when I am more productive than others. I have a date book and a schedule but the time that is mine I organize loosely to create space to putter. I can feel it in my body when there is a shift in my energy. I am hyper-vigilant to recognize my energy and to only allow energy that is for my highest good. That also means noticing when I am absorbing energy around me from people that it is not mine. As I develop my awareness intuitively, I am more acutely aware when I am feeling my mood shift. I am always checking in to see the root of this feeling, emotion. I have learned how to maneuver myself in spaces with people, so I am not a sponge for everyone's moods. It is something I work with my clients. It is a common roadblock for people who are empathic. I am referring to it as a roadblock since I feel it can feel like you are off-roading with someone else's reality.

CHANNEL

Be an answer for your question
Listen to your voice
Speak and be ready to lean into what you know
Do not question what you know for sure
Allow your voice to rise and be true
Know that it is knowledge
Knowledge may lead you to be
Explain less
Be proud and true

See who you are
Know you are enough
Claim a spot of knowing
A knower does not know all
but can take knowledge when offered
take what is offered
it is yours
Make this your own.

We are familiar with clearing the clutter around us. Clearing the clutter of emotions within us is equally important. I find that when I give myself "*puttering* room" every day, it is a time to meander in my mind without a specific focus. To allow our mind to gravitate to what it wants to think about. To sift through thoughts and give myself the time to integrate what needs to be absorbed and let go of what doesn't serve. Get clear with the simple fact that you need this time and give it to yourself. This *puttering* time allows us to process things. We all process things in our own way. If you consider this, you will recognize what you need. This is your sacred time. It is a time for you to reshuffle new information and incorporate what you believe into your life.

AFFIRMATION

Look within to find the voice you seek.

INSPIRATION

Discover your inner value

5

There Is a Voice Inside Us All. Be Still and Listen.

I believe we are meant to have faith in ourselves. That light shines within us so bright that the energy that it holds illuminates our ability to manifest what we are destined to do. Creating the fabric within to cultivate faith in who we are. To trust and know that when we believe in our dreams, we are in fact creating a timeline for it to happen. No outside source can disseminate truth more than our own hearts holding the vision for our dreams. When we realize that we are the conductors to manifest our dreams we begin to realize our innate gifts.

The bravest thing to do is to be still. To listen to my own voice and have that be enough. To remember that I have a light that shines within. This idea is one that's taking me a long time to come to terms with. It seems to me it is easier for me to see the light within other people. To serve them, to show them their light, to show them their purpose and direct them to their soul's path. Several years ago, when I was talking to my mentor, she told me that the best part of my gift is the ability to ask myself what I need to know. It may seem absurd, but I forget from time to time to ask for help. In the beginning I didn't even consider asking anything thinking that I was always meant to ask for others. This idea to connect for me was exciting. I was so thrilled to develop an effortless connection with my guides. I started and stopped so many times feeling like there was a block to my usual effortless connection.

I realized I was thinking too much trying to connect with my thinking mind instead of my heart. I sat with and received a channel that said, "Go to a space that is tranquil within and seek us there." The easiest way for me was to use automatic writing. It has always allowed me to connect at a deeper level. I would sit in my room and take several breaths to create space to receive. Then write a question on a blank sheet of paper in my journal. Initially I got nothing. I kept trying every day. By day four, I started to feel the energy thrum in my body and with my eyes closed I began to write. I never read what I wrote until the next day. It took my breath away at the beautiful responses I received. I did this for months. Here is a sample from one of my earlier downloads or channels.

CHANNEL

Light to who wants knowledge
Show them how to be pure
To who they are meant to be
Ask less
Listen to your voice
Speak and be ready
Lean in to what you know
Do not question what you know for sure
Allow your voice to rise above and be true
Know that it is the knowledge of many that lead you to be
Explain less
Be proud and true
See who you are
Know you are enough
Claims spot of knowing
A knower does not know all
But can take knowledge when offered
The offer is yours
Blank souls do not try to catch something that wants

no strings attached
Work less be joy
Embrace what you believe
Just know to be true
Present in you brings peace to hold
Close to your heart
The peace you search is inside

Now my connection is more visceral, but I take moments every day to tune in to my guides and speak with them. I am always humbled by the information that is presented to me. The truth is that information surrounds us all the time if we open our eyes and our hearts to see it. I think the problem is that many of us are looking for the expert in someone else to define what something means instead of asking ourselves what that means for us and what the universe is actually trying to teach us at this moment.

SOMETHING TO CONSIDER

No matter how far I think I have grown personally, I sometimes still seek validation outside of myself. I am the kind of person who likes to share ideas. When I share my ideas the process of thinking out loud lets me explore these ideas more fully. There is also a part of me that is still seeking acknowledgment that the idea is interesting. Does this make me weak? I think not. I am interested in testing out the parameters of an idea. I always find that when I speak with my friends that my ideas expand and resonate on a deeper level. It also allows for intimacy in relationships. I love having these conversations with my friends. Not every conversation is so intense, but I love knowing I can when I want to. I also revel in the ability to be still, quiet. My favorite thing is when I can "putter." When I am quiet and "putter" about, I get the best information. I get streams of thoughts all the time but while I am moving around my home cleaning or cooking or when I go outside to the garden, I am processing all the messages I get. I find those moments allow me to occupy my thinking mind and allow the information I am receiving to rise up and, in the end, I usually gain more clarity.

The universe wants to provide us with the love and support we desire. We need to stop and pay attention to how to quiet our busy minds so we can hear. Many of my clients tell me they don't know how to quiet their minds. So, I want to be clear I am not suggesting that your mind should be devoid of thought. However, if you find yourself making to-do lists or going over an old conversation, that kind of thinking busies your brain and acts as a block to be in a place to allow new ideas in. I am suggesting when you have these thoughts merely allow yourself to hear all thoughts, and once your mind settles, you will notice you start to let your mind wander. This space is how you begin to listen to what you are receiving.

CHANNEL

The clarity of a moment can shift perspective
Raising high above is a place where the view is plentiful
But the view may be too grand to be understood with a single glance
Have patience
To see what is meant for you
How the universe speaks to you

TAKE ACTION

Take three breaths
Inflate your lungs sigh out the breath and when you open your eyes notice
the first three things you see
What is the message for you?

JUICY NUGGETS

In the midst of a moment you can rise
Raise your vibration
To choose your journey into the next moment
and
Let go of the energy from before
Be connected

AFFIRMATION

I am worthy, I am value

INSPIRATION

See yourself

6

The Events that Transpire Are Here to Help You Gain the Wisdom You Need.

It may seem odd but the lessons we go through teach us the lessons we need to gain wisdom. The first time someone said, "every event has a positive intention," I laughed bitterly inside and said if they knew my stories, they would be quiet.

I have learned that the events in our lives that are the most poignant are not the real teachers. The way we go through these events is what we need to pay attention to. Many people have been through greater struggles than me—there is no way to quantify how someone's pain is measured. Once you start analyzing someone else's experience, you are placing a judgment on them and yourself. How can we judge pain and sorrow? It is a personal journey to understand what the situations you've faced have taught you. When we step away from judgment and allow ourselves to move away from victimhood, we allow ourselves to grieve the dreams we lost and to heal.

In one of my first sessions with my mentor, she told me that my mother dying was a gift. I promptly got up and left the session. After ruminating about what she said I decided I needed to understand what could make a compassionate person say a crazy statement like this. She told me it was a gift because I learned how to count on myself. I learned how to believe in the spirit, and to do things because I believed in them. I wish it all happened so smoothly. That I believed in myself so much that it would have drowned out all the voices I confronted. I know now that my path was to discover my worth, value, and trust in myself because of what I experienced. That it was something I had to uncover inside of me. No one could have told me I had it. There were many moments of self-doubt and feeling bullied by peers. Many times, I wished I were someone else. Still, in all, I believed I was here for a reason. I also learned quickly that victimhood doesn't accomplish anything. Feeling sorry for ourselves doesn't fix anything.

In third grade I found myself the victim of bullying. I couldn't take a step without someone stepping on the heel of my shoe or tripping me. This girl in my class was cruel, pulling my hair and slinging nasty words my way. I was always feeling like I was on the brink of tears. I hated school. I told my sister, who was nine years older, and her advice was to ignore them. I was so different from her, and I was also nine years younger. Although I knew she loved me, she had her own stuff going on. She was married by the time I was thirteen and I didn't think she understood. My parents pretty much said the same thing. My teacher caught me crying and eventually sent me to the guidance counselor. I didn't know what to say to her. I remember sitting across from her with her hair cropped short in a plaid dress and her hands folded on top of her desk. She was reading something while I sat across from her. Her room was tiny. I remember thinking, *why am I here?* I didn't do anything wrong. I kept going to her office a couple of times a week. She would ask me questions, but I didn't share. I felt like I was betraying my dad and my family.

One day I knew I had to share something, so I told her about my mother who had died. I told her about my new brother. In the meantime, I kept telling my parents to switch my class and move to a new school. One day I found out my parents needed to go speak with her. The next thing I knew I got my wish. They said I could change classes. My teacher said, "You can go if you like but don't let them make you leave." I stayed and finally it stopped. Years later I experienced this on the block where I lived. This time it didn't stop and influenced who I socialized with. It was this constant awkwardness all through junior high and high school. They were the popular kids and I steered clear of them. It made me feel less than. In those days it felt so important to be part of a group. I remember my dad and I were on a walk with my dog, and he said some blossoms open fast and others take longer to bloom. The flowers that take longer to bloom last longer and shine brighter. I understood what he was saying but at that moment I wanted to bloom already. I was sort of used to it by the time I was in tenth grade. I still had hope that I could find a friend and we could have a connection.

I just got to my seat in the chorus. Mrs. Pierce took her job seriously and she was a character. When she spoke it had a singsong tone. She loved her job and always pushed us to sing our best. She was speaking to the bass section because someone was spitting spitballs. While she was talking to them, and I listened to Mrs. Pierce use these corny anecdotes to entice them to be the "young men" she "knew they were."

My eyes met a girl who was sitting a few rows from mine. She gave me a knowing look and we both inwardly chuckled. She was fighting the need to laugh out loud like me. I remember how we smirked at each other as we left the chorus room and went to our next class. I didn't even know we were in other classes together. I began to watch her because she was so smart and funny in an unobtrusive way. How did I not see her before? I wasn't worthy by the day I approached her, but our friendship naturally developed, and we began to complete each other's sentences. We had a thousand inside jokes. I could speak to her all day long, she understood me, and I was thrilled to meet someone who got me. We shared so many stories, dreams, and our uncanny ability to not be in the popular group. She fortified my strength and conviction in who I was, and I began to believe I was intelligent. She encouraged me to apply to colleges and crossed her fingers for me as we waited to hear. It was the first time I championed what I envisioned for myself. It was the first time I set a course to believe in a bigger version of myself. I knew I had it in me. I felt like my destiny was knocking on the door and I was ready to open the door and step in. My friendship with her taught me to see myself as she did and to believe past what others at home may see. I chose to believe in myself. This step created a trajectory for me to discover my career as a speech pathologist. I became more confident and although my dad used to call me an idealist when I shared my point of view. I didn't have the courage to go on the journey to discover my intuitive side. Instead, I took a different one. I stopped dreaming for myself and began to dream for my family. I never got the memo that I could dream in all directions. My new story was about being a mom, dog mom, wife, sister, and speech pathologist. I got caught up in the day to day of all of those things. Later much later I started to listen to my inner voice, and I knew I needed to explore what was missing. It was up to me to find the missing pieces. To rediscover what I had passion for, what lit me up. I needed to surround myself with people who felt the same. I was *puttering* in the kitchen, coffee cup in my hand, and Chelsea had her head on my foot. Jade was sitting on the couch, and I could hear her snuffling. Maggie was snoring in the den. I was staring out the window and I heard the voices, my guides, told me there was more. You have more. I saw myself speaking to people, sharing, and I could see how joyful I was. I knew I wanted to step into that version of me.

I dreamed big and saw in my mind how that road was going to allow me to get closer to my purpose. I dreamed of writing a book, speaking on stage, and having the opportunity to speak to people globally. I had a deep desire for people to know how special they were. To choose to believe in who they were and dare to dream. I didn't know how; I just knew what I needed to do. Now was the time; I had to find that belief in myself. The only way I could stop this victimhood dance and being bullied was by learning how to choose myself. I stopped trying to please everyone. I stopped trying to be the person everyone liked. I became content with my circle of people and started to stop being with the people who didn't want me. Sounds so matter of fact and simple. *No!* It was very hard! I learned many more lessons along the way. Friends are the family you make. I have made new friends along the way. I'm still lucky enough to have my friends from high school and college in my life. I've watched them achieve many of their dreams and they stood by me celebrating mine. They are my inner posse, the people who I count on, the people I can speak to, the people I can be myself with.

SOMETHING TO CONSIDER

Authenticity is about allowing your voice to be louder than all the voices out there. Remember my old friend Judgment and her sidekick ego? They come to the party uninvited all the time. The difference is now I invite them in. I even offer them a cocktail. What I learned is that those judgments are a part of an old story I still am tossing around. So now when they show up, I invite them in and have a conversation. There are many stories we have going on. Many of these stories keep us safe. They also keep us hidden and stuck. So, honor the story, see it, hear it, and then look at who you are in this moment and ask yourself if this is who you are. If the answer is no, then tell your ego with all the love and compassion you save for your best friend and give it to yourself. Then take a breath and take a small step toward your dream. Trust in you. Don't wait for someone else to see it in you first.

CHANNEL

The energy we call into takes shape in form
many times by deeds that are bestowed upon us
By people who come in our path
There are no coincidences or accidents.
It is a gift
For you
To receive the gift is yours to choose
Once you feel worthy to receive it

The magnitude of what you are accepting
may become apparent later
Worry not
The gift is in the receiving my love
Receive with an open heart
We are not meant to only gift others
The work is allowing your entity to receive

AFFIRMATION

I am resilient

INSPIRATION

Reflecting

7

JUDGMENT WE HOLD FOR OURSELVES IS THE JUDGMENT WE INVITE INTO OUR LIVES.

Holding onto what we fear has a way of inhibiting change. The exact thing we would like to add to our lives requires us to adopt a new perspective and possibly a new habit. Recognizing that you need to shift is an enlightening process and with it comes the resistance to leave things just as they are. We crave safety and familiarity and change shakes all that up. Change can set you free and allow for more abundance. Change can also create anxiety and inner judgment when we are negotiating all the feelings that come up when we learn something new.

If things show up in our lives, then they are here to teach us something. Our soul's journey has created these situations to teach us. Even if we are not sure exactly what the lesson is, it surfaces later in what many people call an "aha" moment.

When I think about who I was when I was younger, I felt I was trying very hard to please this one or that one: my parents, my teachers, my husband, my employer, my clients, my children. I felt like there was always something I should have done better, known more, or been more diligent. I found it all exhausting and it felt like I was always looking to someone to determine if what I was doing was "acceptable" or "enough." Why did it all matter to me what everyone thought? I didn't know how to please myself. It never occurred to me to ask myself what I thought. It seemed like I never even considered checking in with myself. Instead, I was angry when I was living with my parents so much of the time. I had a feeling in my gut I knew I could do more.

I was afraid to challenge my parents. I remember when I was sixteen, I was in a play, and I got a singing solo. My dad would say, "I don't understand why you spend so much time with these things; it will not lead you anywhere. It won't help you in school or in your life." I said, "I love it." I thought that said it all. I trusted myself to audition and trusted myself to take on the role. I had so much fear of telling him how much joy it brought me. How sharing my voice made me happy. How when I was a part of a play, I felt like I was contributing to making something spectacular. So when he came to the show, he told me afterward he couldn't hear me. When I spoke, he couldn't understand. This "adventure," he called it, was a waste of time. I didn't decide to stop including him. I decided never to invite him again. I closed that part of myself off to him. I never shared this with him again. It hurt inside. Here is what I didn't understand until much later. When there is a conflict, it triggers emotion, and we make choices that shape who we are. The people who are in our lives to trigger the conflict are giving us the opportunity to create change within ourselves.

I was brought up to think that the opinion of my elders outweighed mine. I was taught not to ask myself first. I don't think I knew what I thought; the question I had in my mind was, "Am I good enough?" I was very judgmental of myself, always thinking I wasn't doing as much as I could. I became my biggest critic. I learned this—I received this message in a channeled message: *In order to stop attracting judgment from others I needed to stop judging myself and others around me.*

I knew this was true, but I didn't understand what I needed to shift. I discovered that the opposite of judgment was not acceptance; it was compassion. This is a lesson I am continuing to explore. My natural tendency is to take care of the people who I am connected with. I had this belief that my value was in how I pleased the people I loved. If the sum of my actions were good, then I had more worth. (I am cringing while I write this, but it is true). I am cringing because it brings up all my mixed emotions about the connection between love and food.

My stepmother, Gerda, was an amazing chef and baker. She was trained in Vienna, and she was gifted. She was territorial in the kitchen. She did not want me in the kitchen to cook. I watched her cook over the years and learned from watching but she only allowed my brother to cook with her. She had a love-hate relationship with food. She loved to create sumptuous food, but for as long as I can remember, she was on a diet. She hid all the snacks in the house. One day at school the teacher gave us rub and glue and I got this idea. I became the snack detective and found her secret hiding spots. I opened the bags, put some pretzels and chips in a bag, and then glued the pretzels and chips back together. I hid the stash in my room. I always felt so confused by this. I felt like I was stealing in my own house. I always remember thinking how embarrassed I was that I did this. I thought the whole situation was nuts. I knew there was no way I was doing this in my home with my family. I have so many memories of going with my kids to buy homemade pasta and watching them devour it with their fingers dipping each noodle in the Locatelli cheese. They loved it. One of my best memories is eating dinner with my kids and watching TV after in the den. There is something about sitting around the table and catching up on the day. Funny thing is both my kids turned out to be foodies. We still love having a good meal together and then smooshing together on the couch and watching TV. I realize that it is about the dinner being homemade. It is more about that we get to be together and sharing each other's company. Kevin says, "Going out to eat together is my favorite thing to do."

Although my parents are no longer here, I am going through the process of packing up my parents' house, looking through old pictures and treasures that hold so many memories that are filled with mixed emotions. I can see that my perception of my body image was clouded by her perception, and I still struggle with this, quite honestly. One thing I decided when I was in college and away from home was that I was done living like that. I knew when I had children, no matter how I felt, I would provide it all to my children. I wouldn't reward them for good report cards with food nor would I take food away to punish them. In my mind, food, like love, should be abundant. Abundance is not about providing; it is about creating an atmosphere where you know that you can have what you desire. I was beginning to see that I was connecting my value and worth with what I contributed. I finally saw that I had worth just because I was a person. I still had value if I never made another dinner or did another favor. I needed to see that if I couldn't recognize my worth and value, then how could anyone else? I began to take notice and acknowledge who I was. All the things I did around my home and with my family became a habit and I was so scared to stop doing it all because I believed that was how I needed to show up. *The thing that had me stuck in fear was the very thing that would release me from my stuck point.* The fear was rooted in the idea that I couldn't be valuable without all I was doing. I leaned on others to make decisions because I didn't have faith I could do it alone. When I think about it, I am always leaning on someone's input to approve of my ideas. I remember when I was younger, I would share ideas with Gerda, my stepmom. I would disguise my ideas by saying they were someone else's. If she thought they would be interesting, I would be thrilled and know that those ideas were good. I never let on that they were mine. I believed she wouldn't listen with the same open-mindedness if I said, "I have an idea." I always felt she viewed me as being unintelligent and devised this plan when I spoke to her to field my ideas. It always felt that no one took the time to listen.

Eventually I learned that I had good ideas and that I could make them easily and with confidence. It took me a long time before I got better at making decisions as I got older, but the truth is now I don't need someone to make a decision. I like to share ideas to see if people I know may have more information that will allow me to make a better choice. My desire to seek someone's opinion became less. I realized everyone could have an opinion and they may not all be favorable. I had to allow the opinions of others to mean less. The fear of not being good enough to myself had to end. That fear was holding me in place of exploring what else I was capable of. I couldn't grow in a place of perfection. The only way to grow is by learning through my errors. So I needed to look at my mistakes as teachers and misfire in business as a learning ground for me to try again. I needed to surround myself with people in the same work as me who could support all my misfires and help me to see that there is more to learn and explore. The judgment I held so tight was the door that needed to break open to allow for the inspiration to flow in. Our greatest failures are also our greatest gifts. The universe provides us with lessons, and we have to be able to look at the nuances and make magic.

Juicy Nuggets

The opposite of judgment is not acceptance. It is compassion. For a long time, I felt that my life was run by judgment. I came to expect it. I discovered I also dished it out. My mentor Maria had me rethink this pattern. I was talking to her about judgment. I felt like it triggered me at every turn. You know how I mentioned that Judgment had a best buddy whose name is Ego. Well, those were two characters that were big players in my life. So, I wanted to gain a new perspective on this. I was tired of being subject to judgment and being in this constant state of feeling invaluable, unworthy, and not trusting myself. What I figured out was this. The more I judged other people, the more other people would judge me. Now, of course, this also meant no more judging the outfits or what I thought were poor wardrobe choices some celebrities wore. This one was harder to confess. It centered on my day-to-day life at home. Not complaining about a cup on the counter or an unfolded blanket. I must confess some of these things are hard to navigate since everyone's tidiness differs so drastically. I stopped myself and eventually I stopped having these kinds of negative conversations. It just perpetuated negative energy.

CHANNEL

Judgment is a word that dictates
right or wrong before the act has occurred.
If you believe in a system that needs every act to be measured invite a cast
of judgment to be bestowed on you
If you begin to see that a judgment is not warranted
Then the idea needs not to be weighed or measured.
You merely create an idea and put it out into the universe.
Who receives it has their own interpretation and needs.
If we function from our ego
then they will need the validation
to know what others think.
However, dear one, remember
It is not ours to decide
how the others cast their vote.
It is ours to share our ideas
without the fear of judgment that may come.
If we see each idea as a gift from the universe
We have the right to receive them
as they come
and discard what does not serve us.

AFFIRMATION

I am able to receive wisdom

INSPIRATION

Release judgment

8

Let Go of the Judgment and Instead Consider This

I guess you could say that Judgment and I are best buds. We have a history. It seems when I look back at my life, my buddy Judgment was there. So loud and strong in my life. It was at times suffocating. It was until recently that I realized that Judgment had a sidekick called Ego. The thing is, whenever Judgment came to visit, Ego decided to pour salt on the wound. That is how it was for me for a long time. Judgment would knock me out; it was like getting a punch in the gut (although I never literally experienced this). When Judgment showed up, the feelings that set me off were about being valued. Those feelings I pushed away for years seemed to ring out in my mind and it would create a reaction I wasn't proud of. It affected my sense of worth and inner value. It affected how I developed my body image and my need to please. It would come in and seize my confidence, my value, my worth. Over and over again, I pushed it down and thought I was over those feelings. Then, out of nowhere, when I didn't even know it was happening, I got thrown back into those feelings all over again. I felt victimized, picked on. It made me want to get small and hide. Instead, I would secretly rebel and become angry and bitter. My parents didn't understand when I was younger, and I didn't have the wisdom that I have now to be able to have the words to explain it. I am not sharing this for you to feel bad for me but painting a picture of how completely at a loss I was about how to change this predicament.

I grew up in a house with what I thought were many rules and high expectations. I was always trying to do my best working on my handwriting, which always seemed to be too loopy and hard to read. I tried not to feel bad when I made cards for my dad, and he would tell me to rewrite them because he couldn't read them. I still get a tinge of nervousness writing cards because I fear someone will think that it is messy and unreadable. It took me years not to feel bad when someone asked me to speak lower because I have a loud voice. People would tell me to speak using hushed tones. I seemed to attract these comments. I have been told to shop at different stores because I was too big. Each comment made me again feel like a victim in a sappy soliloquy.

One day I was speaking to my mentor, and she said, "What if you are meant to learn from judgment?"

I was speechless. "OK," I said. "How do I do that?"

"What do you think?" she asked.

So I thought about it and realized I married a lawyer whose job is to judge. How hilarious is that? I asked myself, "What is judgment teaching me?" If I allow the opinions of others to shape who I am then I am what they want to see. If I allow others to have their opinions and thank them for their opinion and choose what is true to me, I get to discover what I think, feel, and desire. It sounds simple, but it wasn't. I was so used to allowing outside people to be my conscious I didn't know how to just decide for myself. I actually avoided decisions, letting everyone else decide and going along with the plan someone else constructed. It was safer and I could avoid being called out when things failed. I was unhappy and emotional. I needed to change.

The first thing that needed to change was my need to ask what to do instead of tuning in to what I desired. The time I spent developing my intuitive gifts taught me that other people didn't need to believe what I knew. As soon I put this into action then came sabotage. I started hearing comments from people around me that they thought I knew it all and couldn't listen to anyone else's opinion. My ego was screaming in my ear to lash back and sometimes, quite honestly, I did. I began to see that feeling that what I perceived as judgment was a choice that allowed me to understand where I still needed to grow.

I learned that if I stopped seeing the judgment in others, I could stop attracting it coming to me. It is easy to see the fault in others and harder to comment on what is good. I noticed that although I desired this from others, I wasn't always forthcoming in my appreciation for who they were. I felt like I was starting to see that my need to please stemmed from my need to feel valued.

If in fact I began to see my own value and worth, I had less of a need to seek it from outside of myself. I have tried to steer away from, but I would be lying if I said I don't say, "You left your coffee cup out" to my husband, or speak with judgment to myself and say, "Let's see how the soup I made is; you never know," instead of acknowledging that I made some soup and simply asking, "Do you want some?" We are our biggest critics. I needed to change the language I used to talk about myself. Now, I find myself a quiet observer as much as I can. I am like many people who are more judgmental of themselves and then others. It doesn't bring a feeling of joy or connection. So, I try to catch myself when I do since the energy I attract is not something I desire. It took me a lot of inner work to understand that the way to release judgment is by having more love and compassion for who I am.

AFFIRMATION

I attract what I desire

INSPIRATION

It all starts with loving me

Something to Consider

We have to notice before we can change. Once you remove the judgment, you then can have the freedom to create. The world has become very big and there are so many things to choose from. When doubt comes pouring in when you are making decisions, the person we blame many times is ourselves. We engage in what I call the "shoulda woulda coulda" dance. There are always choices to make but nothing feels worse than casting judgment on yourself and being stuck. Fear of choosing wrong has kept many people stuck. Not trying something because you don't know how it is expected. The difference between feeling stuck and trying is perspective. If we can allow ourselves the ability to not be perfect, then whatever we try is just information. Don't feel like you need to be an expert.

How can you be an expert in something before you've even tried it? Always being in control and feeling as though we need to have all the answers prevents the flow of new information from coming to us from the universe. We create so much pressure on ourselves to achieve something new it is ludicrous. One of the biggest dream-stoppers is worrying about "*how*." I have talked about this a lot in many different groups. My one big takeaway is this: No one can be exceptional at everything. You can learn how to do anything you desire. The question is do you want to. The first thing to do is to look at where you are stuck. Then examine it and see if having support would allow you to accomplish this goal. How do you want to use your creative energy? I heard this idea many times but never realized how freeing this is. To be able to hire an expert while you focus on what you are gifted at is so unbelievably freeing. It allows you to attract positive energy around your work.

CHANNEL

Giving permission to allow yourself
to step into who you believe, who you desire to be
It is the shining moment where you get to clear who you simply are
without holding the energy of how
by doing that
you let go holding on (to the) energy for the people in your life
we are the door, but the truth is, my sweet,
you were holding their energy for too long
holding them captive in their own maturation and fear
of owning what was is theirs
It theirs
It is—their burden
was not yours to carry
gently giving it back to them with love and compassion
to hold them the most capable of being
able to manage and see to their own souls or destiny
to see and release what they desire in their life
It is part of their life's work and life's destiny
continuing to hold it for them prevents them from feeling the pain
releasing the judgment of all the years that they've held onto
holding their value against what they were doing
instead of seeing that their value is who they are
we are all reapers of the earth of the planet
the energy that we hold attracts energies to us
that are like in similar energy
no longer to attract people who can show you your worth
your energy is now
to attract people who discovered or want to discover their own
white buffalo calf woman

AFFIRMATION

I create the energy I want to attract

INSPIRATION

Healing heart inspiration

9

We Must Change Our Energy to Change Our Lives.

Create a positive, loving environment. We create clusters of connections. Do you ever notice when you meet a person who you resonate with because of who you both are? There have been times in my life when I meet a new person and it feels like I already know them. Our relationship feels like we have picked it up after not seeing each other for a few months or years. These friendships are effortless and evolve so easily and I feel like they already know me. I used to think I needed to guard myself from allowing my heart to trust these people. My instinct said it is safe to trust it. The truth was I second-guessed myself for a long time. I never forgave myself for not listening to my sister tell me not to trust my stepmother. I was little and thought this felt safe. It was a difficult relationship, and still now, after Gerda, my stepmother, passed away, I am still healing from that decision that little girl of four made. I have forgiven that little girl and even told her she made the best decision she could have made. I think I figured out that Gerda taught me how to begin to rely on myself and to trust in what I wanted. I needed to believe it and then work to achieve it.

I have found in this process of becoming an intuitive life coach. The people I call my friends are people who I call seekers. They have a desire to live each moment authentically. They are connected to how they want to live their life. These people who I call my friends are motivated to experience life fully. They have chosen to find a way to choose the way they want to live. When you think that you can choose how you want your life to unfold, you come from a different motivation. Having passion in your work, relationships, and in the way you face your day you create positive momentum. I didn't actively seek people like this, but when I look at the people I engage with, I can see a common thread. I attracted people who wanted similar things. There was a time I befriended people who were parents of my kids' friends, and those friendships were important, but the common interest was that we were parents. I have a group of women I have known from high school and college and those women have emerged as creative, intelligent women who have inner strength and I adore each one of them.

The friends I have met more recently support and have my back through all of my inner growth and accepted me as an intuitive long before I did. They saw in me what I couldn't see and nurtured all my steps.

There are the people in your life you are born to and people you choose to surround yourself with. It becomes the family you make. When I began to shift the people, the conversations I had with people shifted. We attract who we desire to be surrounded with. The people who you are with should allow you to be your most authentic self. Discovering spaces where I can be who I am allows me to continue to be inspired and supported. Our families are where we live, and our friendships, I have found, are where I have grown.

CHANNEL

Giving permission to allow yourself
to step into who you believe you desire to be
is your shining moment
where are you
get to clear who you simply are
without holding the energy of how
by doing that
you may not be holding energy for the people in your life
we are the door—but the truth is
my sweet, you were holding their energy for too long

holding them captive
in their own immaturity
and fear of owning what was theirs
It theirs
It is and their burden
not in yours to carry
and gently
give it back to them with love and compassion
to hold them the most capable
of being able to manage and see to their own soul or destiny
to see and release what they desire in their life
is part of their life's work and life's destiny
continuing to hold it for them
prevents them from feeling the pain and releasing the judgment
of all the years that they've held onto
holding their value against what they were doing
instead of seeing that their value wasn't who they are
we are all reapers of the earth and of the planet
the energy that we hold attracts energies to us
that are like your energy
It is no longer to attract people who can show you your worth
your energy is now to attract people
who discovered or want to discover their own
White Buffalo Calf Woman

AFFIRMATION

In every moment, I have compassion for who I am

INSPIRATION

Abundance lies within

10

POSITIVITY IS PRACTICE,
NOT A PLACE TO GET TO.

A positive state of mind can dim the negative voices. Love finds you when you find it in yourself. In order to share love with another person, first you need to find love for who you are. I have heard this anecdote many times. I even thought I understood it. The truth is owning who you are and accepting all the parts of you sounds easier than it is.

Have you ever noticed that people actually enjoy being negative? It gives them a reason to harness their anger. That kind of group consciousness attracts negative thinking and perpetuates anger, frustration, and judgment; it never really has a warm and fuzzy outcome. The people who just can't help complaining about things also find it easier to find fault in themselves as well as with others. They seem to pride themselves on their ability to point out what others are overlooking in their actions. They are also the ones that have difficulty believing in their worth and value and find it hard to trust. There are many who have been down this road and from time to time find themselves dwelling in negativity only to find themselves in this spiral that continues to notice more negativity. In the end it leaves us all feeling pretty dismal.

In order to shift out of this perspective and stop participating in the negative conversation, you need to consider that what you seek will come. If you go out searching for what is less than perfect, you will no doubt find it. If you are like me, you have found that this approach has not resulted in any kind of positive outcome. Instead it has left you feeling blue, unfulfilled, and without hope. I was in the muck. Negative conversations are everywhere—in the news, social media, and conversations with our family. With the quarantine of 2020 and COVID-19, I had to stretch to choose to see it another way. I could not go anywhere without hearing every dismal outcome, endless numbers and scenarios.

I decided to stop. Change the information I was attracting. I know you are thinking, *how do you just stop?* It is a choice, just like other choices we make to drink less coffee or turn our phones off at a certain hour. I just felt called to try this on.

If we consider that we can choose each moment and how we can respond. If we actually do not allow ourselves to go forward in time, we can be in the now moment. This is the practice that has allowed me to release anxiety and take a breath to see possibility in every moment. I realize this approach seems illogical when planning. So let me explain. The things I choose to focus on are where I put my energy. I found myself being pulled out of my present state and into a negative tailspin and then getting annoyed once I realized I was down the rabbit hole. I was opening myself up to conversations and ideas that I did not want to engage in. The result was that I felt the effects showing in my mood and my productivity in my day. I started to make rules about what I wanted to discuss and what I didn't and turned off the TV so I wasn't exposed to the perpetual information on all the news channels. I remember coming downstairs and there was Kevin, making an innocent cup of coffee. I came into the room and without even a "hi honey," I began to complain about the noise and turned off the TV and Alexa, who was blaring music. It wasn't just the volume of noise; it was that they were announcing somebody who was killed, or some tragic news story and I was hit with all the emotions that those stories bring up before I even had a sip of coffee. It never dawned on me that he was just living his life, noise and all. It was too much for me. I shut down the conversations while we ate, and they were rehashing the news stories of the day.

Then I realized that controlling everything around me was like living in a dictatorship. So as much as I don't enjoy it, I cannot ask everyone else to live like me. I will say now Kevin plays meditation music instead of the news. I have learned not to put my earbuds in my ears and shut them out but instead to use the time they are speaking about things I don't enjoy as an invitation to daydream.

Now, I can see that I can simply choose not to engage. When I feel triggered in a situation, it is more complicated. I have come to learn that triggers are like little spotlights to learn about something unresolved within myself. Do you ever notice that when you are in a situation where there is conflict, after all the eloquent words you wanted to say come pouring in? Under defensiveness, vulnerability, and judgment is usually the message you are meant to discover. I would be lying if I told you I always figure it out and deconstruct the whole conversation to get to the part where I was triggered and then discern the spot where the nugget of a lesson lies. I try and sometimes succeed on my own, but I have reached out and asked my guides for help and that always provides me with the affirmations I need to move forward. I also ask a coach I am working with or one of my trusted friends. This enterprise of personal growth should not be taken lightly. Once you begin and you get the excavator out, you are in for the long haul. It enables you to become your great ally. Standing up for yourself to create loving boundaries. To be with people I want to be with. Have conversations with people who light me up. I create boundaries and share when I no longer want to discuss them. I was nervous about creating boundaries, but I find that the more I do this, the more comfortable I am.

I am focused on creating my attention on things that will improve my day. It is a choice. I can say I choose to listen and have conversations with people I want to engage in. We have free will to choose what suits us. Understand that the universe is there for all of us. It doesn't show favoritism.

Juicy Nuggets

If we think of ourselves as if we were a banana, we will truly understand that our outer shell, or peel, in this case, allows us to stay safe. It also inhibits us from feeling pain and living in it. When you have a shield up, it creates a barrier between the good and bad. So to start to peel our layers back, we have to appreciate our worth and value. So we can create a place to live and be who we really are. I say remember because our higher selves know our value and worth. We have forgotten by allowing the information of others and believe what they say as being true.

Here are five steps to use in your awakening:

Step 1. Grant ourselves permission to be who we are.

Step 2. Trusting ourselves and our inner knowing.

Step 3. Receiving information to allow us to grow. To be in a space to accept support from people and see where you are attracting abundance in love and friendship.

Step 4. Letting go of the judgment we hold from our ego and the voices from past wounds.

Step 5. Allowance and reconnection to yourself.

These are the steps I used and use with my clients to allow for inner growth and the discovery of our inner selves.

Channel

Hold tight to the belief
the notion that each of us
has the right to discover our true self
we cannot hand it to each other
like you would a treasure stone.
We need to have faith and trust
in them to discover who they are
the inner work needs to be done
to discover what drives us

Is revealed by living day to day
in the mundane activities of life
many of us feel as though
we stumble upon our gifts
having no memory
when the exact moment was when
we discovered our gift
it is gently pet placed within our soul
emerges when we are ready to see it.
Each of us discovering
coveting our gifts as the true treasures they are
It is free will that propels us forward to
Step into who we are with courage

AFFIRMATION

I choose positivity

INSPIRATION

Attracting the positive

11

LISTEN TO YOUR INTUITION.
IF SOMETHING DOESN'T FEEL
RIGHT—IT JUST ISN'T RIGHT.

Don't ignore that first instinct. Your intuition cuts past your ego to recognize what you need. Being positive is an action you choose each day. It is a choice to see that you are where you are meant to be and how you want it to be and feel at each moment.

I always tell people who ask that grad school has no fluff. There are no light and easy classes. It felt like every moment counted and the urgency to get it all in my brain was intense. We all knew how hard it was to get a spot in the program, and to stay, it meant we had to do well. I was in a constant state of worry. The weight of finals was in every breath I took. I felt that no amount of time could ever be enough to prepare me. One day when I was coming from the clinic, I saw a friend who looked awful. I asked her to have coffee with me. So, we bundled up to walk across the campus for coffee in the hopes that it would not only give me unbridled energy but also allow me to stay focused.

We trudged across the campus in silence and finally she said, "I can't get this stuff. I am gonna fail. How will I graduate and get married on time?"

As she continued to trudge across the field in the snow, I looked at her and started to laugh nervously, then I mumbled, "OK, you're right! I agree; let's just give it all up!" Then I confessed, "I am hanging on by a thread too."

Her eyes widened in disbelief, and I shared how hard it was to commute to my internship and how living at home was not easy. I confessed that I worried I wasn't smart enough to retain all this information. I just wasn't sure how I was going to make this all work. Then she stared back at me. I think I confused her; she thought I was going to give her a pep talk.

Then I said, "What if we aren't supposed to know it all? Maybe we are meant to figure it out." I confessed that I tried to remember why I was doing this to myself, working so hard. Then I said, "I think of giving it up and I feel sad because I actually believe I can help people." I shared how my dad thought I was idealistic. I blinked away tears and shared that I believe that everyone needs to be able to be heard. She looked at me and blinked tears away too. We both continued to move gingerly in the snow. We got our coffee and splurged on a cookie. We dusted the snow off a bench and sat down on a cold afternoon, looking at the smoke twirling in the air with snow flurries blowing around us. We talked about what we wanted to do after grad school. We remembered why we signed up for all the craziness anyway. We walked into the final feeling way better. We made a choice at that moment to remember our dream and to choose it over our fear. We never spoke about that day, but I saw her in January when classes started, and we both knew we had passed. I learned something that day. I needed to stay on the course I set because I had a bigger dream than just getting a degree. I wanted to help children speak. I used that energy to steer me past the fear of writing a thesis or getting an internship. I knew in my gut there would be bigger things coming and I could use that energy of fear to direct me, or I could decide to stay in the moment I was in and not worry about new ones. I could not control it all.

The thought that I was in control of how things played out sat in the front of my mind. This idea that I alone could change the outcome boggled my thoughts. It is more than the cup is half full or half empty. It is allowing the universe to lead and recognizing that, in every moment, it is exactly where you are meant to be. Having faith and trust that it is indeed what it is supposed to be. I am not going to delve into any spiritual practices because anything and everything we do that brings us peace and an opportunity to further align with our authentic selves is, in my mind, perfect.

The idea of choosing to live in the moment. Decide that you can create the moments in your day and take information that is in front of you as signs about your path or choices you get to make. If you are in a situation where there is traffic, you can decide to get frustrated or you can decide to live in the moment and make the best of it. What meaning are you willing to make out to the situations that come before you?

CHANNEL

Smile to many and see the world respond in "KIND."
Looking at people
as you walk by with a smile
Providing light and positivity.

AFFIRMATION

I choose to be positive

INSPIRATION

Connection is only a breath away

12

WHEN YOU FEEL LIKE
YOU ARE ON REPEAT,
IT IS BECAUSE YOU ARE.

We experience the same lessons until we gain wisdom from them. It is karma loop 101.

I call this phenomenon a "rerun" and feel like I was stuck in a rerun pattern in my life for so long.

I found myself in situations with friends that were agreeable one too many times. I was the go-with-the-flow person. The truth was many times I didn't care, but most of the time, I didn't want to get into a situation of negotiations. Later, I discovered those friendships were many times surface friendships. I didn't want to share my needs and preferences and by withholding them they really never knew me. In return I created a wall and didn't let people get to know me. I was standing in judgment of myself and wanted to be part of the group at any cost instead of being alone. To no surprise, these friendships fizzled out.

So how do we make ourselves ready to end the "rerun"?

In order to start to take in the information, the universe is showing us we need to be able to see the information as a teacher. Many situations have come up in my life where I thought by remaining quiet and "going with the flow," everything would be easier. I was worried about being judged for my opinion. I was used to pushing down my voice to create a harmonious situation. *I did* have opinions about lots of things. I got so used to thinking that others' opinions were better than mine or more popular I stopped listening to my own. I would stand in the kitchen with my stepmother while we cleaned up from dinner and try to share but I was so fearful of her knocking down my ideas and dreams. I was very careful sharing what I thought since most of the time I was told these ideas were idealistic, not well thought out, or that I didn't have what it took to accomplish them. My home was pretty traditional, and on Friday night we had dinner in the dining room. The table was set with the good dishes and my mom taught me how to fold the napkins, so the table looked festive. We used the good glasses from the China cabinet. The Shabbat candles were lit. There was always an appetizer or soup and an entree served family-style with a starch and vegetables. My mom was a trained baker and chef so there was always something special. My brother always served the drinks, and my mother and I cleared and brought out the new food. After dinner my dad and brother would go to the den. I put away the leftovers and stayed in the kitchen while my mom did the dishes that couldn't go in the dishwasher. One day I had this idea I was thinking about—teach an after-school class sponsored by the Y I worked at in the summer. I knew the director and they had talked to me during the summer about possibly teaching during the year. I wasn't sure then I thought it would be fun to do this with my friend and make some money too. I had an idea for an art class for elementary kids. I remember telling my mom it was my friend's idea to do these art projects as an after-school class. That my friend thought it would be great if every week they left making one thing. I shared how I liked this idea too. I hoped she could do it in the fall. My mom thought it sounded good and that keeping the projects simple would help make it fun. I felt so happy she liked this idea, but I didn't have the courage to say it was my idea because I was afraid. I still was seeking some acknowledgment that I had a good idea. This was my way of sharing by disguising what I was thinking and dreaming. I didn't know how to just have a conversation. Everything always felt like a test.

My dad started a routine when I was twelve. On Friday we ate together for Shabbat, so he thought it would be a good time to teach me about the world. He gave me an article on Tuesday to become familiar with and we would discuss it at dinner. I would get stomachaches because it was like being in school. My dad had good intentions. He was very intelligent, but I felt so inadequate for these conversations. I did not understand world politics or investments. He would listen and try to take in all he was saying but by no means was this a conversation. I could not share how difficult this was for me. I could not share my real opinions if they differed from his. That is what I believed. As I got older and into my college years, I started to share more of my opinions but again it was not met kindly, and I learned to be quiet. I silently felt *he doesn't understand me*. It made me feel like I didn't belong, and I wasn't understood or accepted. It took me a long time to see that I didn't need to have him approve of all my actions. It still hurt when he didn't approve of the things that I did that were valuable. It caused countless arguments with my husband. Going to my dad's home was stressful, and I felt like I was holding my breath until there was a conflict. My dad at ninety-five still enjoyed about politics, investments, religion, and spirituality. Many times he looked to Kevin to have some meaty discussion about global politics or a trending story in the news.

Many times I felt like my dad and I were on the brink of a huge conflict. I tended to shy away from these scenes for as long as I could remember, afraid of the confrontation.

When my dad met Kevin, he was not a big fan. He couldn't actually say anything negative about him as a person. He did not care for the way he dressed and that he didn't formally greet him and shake his hand. I remember asking Kevin to wear better pants to shake his hand. Kevin was who he was, and he wasn't going to change who he was. I actually respected him for it. I found out years later that my dad did too. In the thick of it all I wanted to do was change him. I was so used to changing myself for my dad or simply not being authentic with my dad.

We had been dating for three years and when we got engaged my dad still didn't approve. It hurt me because I knew who the man I was marrying was and I loved him. I wanted my dad to see it too. My dad was asking me why Kevin doesn't shave on the weekends. I said he does it every day for work. He felt it was a lack of respect to not shave when he was coming to the house and would see him. With every explanation I could feel my temper flaring. I didn't know how to explain it. It dawned on me that by being defensive I was communicating that there was something to defend. So I stopped responding. My dad would make a comment and I would not respond. It became easier and easier. He didn't stop and I continued not to answer.

On my wedding day during the father/daughter dance, my father said, "I want it all for you. I hope I gave you all the things you needed. I married so quickly to give you a mom and a complete life. I want you to be happy." He kissed me. As the tear trickled down my face, I saw him. I understood that he wanted the best for me. He just didn't know how to tie it up in a pretty bow. I began to see there was more there.

Flash forward thirty years, my dad was in the hospital and my husband came to meet me there. My dad told Kevin he didn't need to visit him. Kevin said, "I came to meet Robin." My dad blinked. My husband had my back. My dad called me the next day and said, "I am glad you married Kevin; he was a good choice." I laughed and said, "Yes, Dad, I always knew he was." When I hung up the phone, I chuckled to myself and thought, *good thing I didn't wait for his approval.* I knew deep down in my gut that Kevin and I were right for each other. Lessons come to us all the time but what we are ready to see and hear change as we change.

Channel I Received
After My Dad Passed

In the spark of a whisper
I can hear the breath of those that are near
the energy they transmit to me seems to seep into my bones
into my mind into the very being that I am
brings me a sense of connection and interconnection

into the time in space that I am in, in the here and the now
how that energy transposes into different timelines
yet it still connects to me love
it does not disappear, nor does it get erased
it goes into others into the ethers of your mind
then it allows you to feel it in the depths of your soul
every emotion that you feel every breath that you take
it invites us to revitalize ourselves
all the steps that we are thinking about
stop thinking
allow yourself to be in this space
allow it to bring new meaning without finding it
allow it to bring comfort to your heart without questioning it
allow it to bring meaning to your soul without wondering
who's bringing it in
o be in a place of receiving all that is coming to you
and know that your soul family has risen up to bring you comfort
from the many timelines that you have been in your life
and the timelines that you have lived in
In the here and now, know where you are
at this moment they are coming forward to bring you support
love and light all you need to do is accept it all
I need to accept it and surrender to what is coming to me
and know that it is mine to receive
and carry that love and light into my heart
as I meander through the day
in the spark of a whisper I can hear the breath of those that are near
the energy that they transmit seems to be seeping into my bones
into my mind into the very being that I am
and it brings me a sense of connection and interconnection
into the time and space that I am in in the here and now
in an hour where I seek light, I receive all
the energy transposes into different timelines
and yet it all connects back to me love does not disappear

nor does it get it erased
it goes into either of your mind
and it allows you to feel it in the depths of your soul
and every motion that you make
every breath that you take

A MESSAGE FOR YOU

Reruns happen when we aren't absorbing the lesson we need to learn from a situation. Lessons repeat when we are in a place of holding onto what our egos are reacting to instead of absorbing what the situation that has presented is teaching us. Things happen over and over because the universe keeps presenting the same circumstances hoping that we will see and change. How many times do you drive down a street and not notice a specific sign or tree? We don't see until we are ready to absorb the information.

So when a trigger finds you and you want to scream, "Not this again!", next time ask yourself what the message is for you. Triggers and reruns are the universe shining a spotlight on us. Growth happens when we stop pushing back from the information. Our ego wants to hold us in judgment but then we cannot see or hear. We have to receive the information and let our intuition play detective and figure out what the message is. Mistakes are only mistakes when we cannot forgive ourselves.

AFFIRMATION

Triggers that happen in my life are teachers

INSPIRATION

Change your vibration

13

My Body Is a Reflection of My Mind

It takes only one person to change your life—*you*.

The most destructive thing you can do is tear yourself down. Yet it seems that it is something I confess I was very good at. I still catch myself from time to time sitting in my old story and this was the story loop I played. I hope I can _____. That word *hope* actually implies that there is a chance that what you desire has the possibility of not happening! I hear my clients say this all the time. It was a big stretch for me to acknowledge that when I say I hope someplace in my mind I am holding onto the notion that I don't believe in my affirmation or dream. In some upside-down world I imagined that using the word *hope* was like getting a jail-free card in Monopoly. My story went like this: when I use the word "hope," I am thinking positive thoughts of what I desire, when the truth is *hope* also allows me to not get fully invested in what I was committing to. It allows room for failure. I know this may sound nit-picky but people in a championship game are not saying in a huddle, "I *hope* we win." "I hope I win," said no Olympic athlete ever. They are declaring that they will be the champions. I noticed when I changed the conversation from, "I hope I write a book" to "I am writing a book." I started showing up to make it happen. I realized as I explored this further that although I signed up to be part of inspirational women who have created inspirational ideas. I was excited and attended all the meetings and I still had doubts surfacing, tapping me on the shoulder, waking me up at night. Those doubts were buried deep in the nooks and crannies of my subconscious and although I was willing to do the work, I didn't know how to reach the spot where they called home and let them go. The importance of letting them go was that I needed to create a new story and conquer this idea I had that I didn't have what it took to be a writer and that my story wasn't worthy of telling. Then I heard this:

CHANNEL

See your light through the light of another
Let their light guide you
Let it be a mirror of who can choose to be
Allow it to feed your tattered ego
Bring you light
So you can hear the messages
meant for you to share
Be a vessel
Share the light
For another's eyes
To see witness in them

I felt like I was beginning to see. I realized that the battle for me to see who I was was for me to surrender to this. Battles that confront us in our lives are never chosen. They seem to appear. It is up to us to be warriors and deconstruct the mental blocks we have built. To allow us to step into who we are meant to be. It didn't matter how many coaching sessions I had. I needed to rewrite my belief of what I actually could do, discover my value and worth and then go about sharing my wisdom with you. I held onto this mission in an effort for people thinking to rediscover infinite wisdom. I was stuck. I knew it was a big shift for me to do this and the only way was through. I needed to let go of this. I did many things and it all allowed me to get closer to where the issue was, but when I started to do breathwork, I was able to get to a new level of release.

A friend of mine kept talking about breathwork. I thought, *OK, I need to try this.* So I signed up. I lay on the floor, listening to the instructor lead me through the breathing technique. He asked us to let go and forgive our parents for not being enough for us. They did their best. I started to weep. I realized how much judgment I held in my body. After I was so exhausted and discovered how much lighter I felt. I kept showing up. Every week he guided us through another session, releasing old stagnant information I had buried. I discovered I was able to connect to my guides easier. I was able to work on my relationship with my dad with grace. I was able to let go of the buried emotions I stashed in my body. I felt a sense of oneness. I felt lighter and able to sustain a higher frequency. I was more creative and able to let go of the judgment I was holding onto about not being enough. That my value came from how I viewed myself, not what others felt about me. I began to understand that if I give permission to allow another person to take away my power, beauty, and wisdom, they can. That I can choose at every moment to hear it and not absorb the comments. I said many times when I was younger that I wished the negative comments could slide off me. Well, when I am in the right frame of mind and holding love and compassion for me first, then I am Teflon. The wisdom I hold is mine and who I attract to share it with chooses to consider what I am thinking. Looking for magic? It's in you. There is no one who is more magical than you! We have the power inside us. We each get to choose our wisdom and believe in it. We can be magical.

CHANNEL

Let go let go of the ideas
that have knitted into your mind
that I've allowed you to craft a story
about who you actually are
Do they come from someone else's perspective
another set of eyes

another viewpoint
another story
if you were to let them go
who would you be
could you craft a new story
who you are we
with the out those eyes of another
looking on
you could be anything
Let it take shape in your mind
you can be what you dream
could you allow your mind to meander
into all the things that you could be
all the things that you can't even see with clarity
Things you can only sense
Let go of the judgments
They hold us back
from the allowing our minds to expand
consider all that we can be
Those judgments were not meant
To hold us back
they were meant to be a guide
even a spotlight
to see where we need to expand
When we were young
they were meant to keep us safe
our young minds misread them
misunderstood those ideas
the people who looked upon us
gave us rules
how they believed we needed to live our lives
what if they were merely suggestions
to keep us safe in the moment
we are not those little ones anymore

we are in a new place on a new timeline
we get to craft the stories
that we want to dream
That we want to live
Live our daydream

AFFIRMATION

I am magical, I have wisdom, I have value

INSPIRATION

It all starts with sending love to you

14

We Gain Wisdom and Purpose during the Greatest Emotional Loss and Turmoil.

I've known since I was little that death is a part of life. I remember thinking you can't have one without the other. My mother died when I was three and we seldom discussed her life. It seemed the conversation was always about how she died. I didn't understand why everyone was trying to understand how come—why now—when what they wanted to know was why did I have to lose her. Their pain was personal, and the pain was too great to encapsulate into a story. They hold on to that pain as their lasting connection to who they lost. My dad held his pain close to his heart, never sharing anything about who my mother was when she was alive. There were no pictures shared although he had many. He very seldom shared any stories of their life together. In the last months he was alive I would go to his house. I would sit next to him at the dining room table and hold his hand very gently. His fingers were swollen and stiff from arthritis. At this point he was worried about dying; he could feel it was close. My brother and sister reassured him that we would be OK. This one particular day he said, "Later, I won't be in your mind." I said, "It is all in the memories and stories, Dad." It struck me then how he worried he was worried he would be forgotten. So, I told him that his energy was knitted into mine and that I couldn't forget him without forgetting who I was. His children were his legacy.

I am cleaning out his home. I found all his cherished memories in boxes. Mementos from the life he had. I wished he could have shared his stories to go with them. My mother-in-law told me a long time ago that he needed to hold on to his memories; it was all he had left. I began to understand.

I used to wonder if once you died that was all there was to talk about. We visited my mother's grave two times a year and manicured the tree on the plot in front of her gravestone. It was just the three of us. We left very early and drove about ninety minutes. The three of us took turns cutting the hedges and clearing out the weeds. My dad became so quiet and almost reverent in his own memories. After we cleared everything, it was time to find a stone for her grave. I would walk off beyond the other gravestones to find the perfect rock. I dug my nails into the earth to retrieve the stone I spotted. Not caring that my nails would have dirt encased in them from the cemetery. I tried not to think about the earth that was there and what it was made from. It sort of freaked me out. In the Jewish religion we place a rock on a gravestone to honor the person who has passed as a way of saying we remember you. I would say a special message to her as I placed the rock on her stone. As I did it each time, I felt conflicted. I always felt her essence was not there.

I had a faint memory from long ago when I was three. I knew when she passed away before my dad asked me to kiss her goodbye. I don't remember much except that he let me go on their bed with my red shoes on. I saw the scene unfold in my mind; the way I moved slowly, crawling next to her on the big bed. I loved holding her hand and how she always held mine loosely, trusting me to go and knowing I would always come back. Now her hand was limp and did not curl around my fingers. It felt so strange, like I had lost the connection to her. She was no longer there. I couldn't understand what I was looking at, her hair was all matted, but her face was quiet. Yet she didn't feel like she was there anymore. She was in her bedroom right next to mine. All her things were all around her. Her body was there. She was not. I felt so confused, not sure why my dad looked so sad. I knew I had to make him smile again. My sister was acting odd too. I didn't understand.

To me, my mother was someone I spoke to in spirit form. I spoke to her whenever I wanted while I walked to school or played with my dolls. During these times the connection to her felt real. The feeling at her grave was emptiness. I thought it was because I was so little when she passed. I realized that what I was seeking was the essence of who she was. I had no memories to retrieve that made me feel closer to her. I tried to ask for information from my sister and my dad. I found these conversations awkward and painful. So, I began to ask my spiritual guides that I connect to and who provide wisdom to me to help me find evidence of my own. My dad and brother gave me pictures of me with my mom. I sat with them and connected to me as a little girl and saw the love and trust I had with my mom. I took in all the nuances in the pictures and connected to how cherished I was. This helped me to connect to her. I have to confess that the connection to her is still not strong for me when I am at her grave. I am gifted with the essence of her energy from time to time. Mostly I feel it as a soft breeze on my skin.

The fear of death is not so much that we will die but about what our legacy will be. How will we be remembered by the people who mattered most to us? For the people who are left behind, the fear is how I can hold onto the memory of the person's voice, touch, gaze, and laugh. "Inside each of us we harbor a spot in our hearts where those memories are implanted so we can hold onto the very essence of the person we lost." What I have come to understand is the openness of conversation about how a person lived, their idiosyncrasies and how they made us feel and how they made us feel is what we need to share and hold onto. Instead of creating opportunities to talk about people who we have lost, we need to weave those stories about them into the everyday fabric of our lives. Effortless action.

When I met my husband, I could immediately feel the connection between him and his mother. I knew that when the time came, it would be up to me to teach him how to create a living memory of her. Years later, when my mother-in-law was ill, I began to place pictures around my house of her and my kids. These pictures were not posed portraits; they were fun and showed her interwoven into our lives. I began sharing stories about how she liked a cup of coffee with her hamburger and slice of raw onion and her failed attempt at making stuffing. My husband and I spoke about her quirks and chuckled with our kids all the time in this effortless way indicating to our kids that the conversation was available at any time. I wanted my husband and children to have memories that were familiar so they could have a way to remember her and always know how she adored them. This approach has created a way for us to always feel like we can talk about her and even laugh. When we begin to create living evidence, we are continuing the relationship we had with the person who passed. We are connected to her spirit and that connection brought more love and compassion into our hearts. It allowed us to remember how special she was and to share how our lives were forever changed because of the love she gave so freely. Her open acceptance and non-judgmental attitude were liberating and inviting. I adored her.

The conversations we have about people we love are what foster the ongoing connection. The freedom to speak about people who passed was so important to me. The only conversations we had were about how my mother became ill and how she suffered when she died. My mother was the love of Dad's life and holding onto all of her was his way of keeping her close. He didn't realize that not sharing his memories of her with me didn't allow me to form my own connection in a living memory.

Creating the foundation of these conversations in your family is what keeps the ones we love relevant and allows their memories to continue to flourish.

CHANNEL

It is not in the small things [we hold onto or] that we see in the trinkets
we procure
They do (not) contain the essences or spirit of the people we lost
But we hold those things close
Since (we) rediscover our connection
we cherish them
We cling to the memories
that we created in a time
where things were new and fresh
We hold onto the treasures
as though they were a string that connects us
The biggest fear
is the loss of the connection
always knowing
holding on to the thread
that connects us
to those who are not here in body anymore

AFFIRMATION

I am a conduit to create a living legacy of those I love

INSPIRATION

You are a gift

15

Every Phase in Life Showers Wisdom, Even Death.

It was the fall and my sister and I were going to go bike riding. We were in the driveway, about to pull away. When my parents' car pulled up, my mom was carrying a puppy. I dropped everything. I had wanted a pet for what seemed like forever. I was in love. I ran upstairs to give her one of my dolls. We named her Rhoda after Mary Tyler Moore's funny friend. She was going to be my friend and I adored her. I snuck her into my bed when no one was around. I used to scrap her nails on my parents' door at night when they locked her out so they would let her in. I loved having her around. We were so connected. I felt so fortunate to have her in my life.

So when my family moved into a home, I knew we would get a dog eventually. My cats were getting older. I adopted Dezi as a father's gift for Kevin after we got married. He was more like a dog than a cat. He came when I called and would talk to me and ask for turkey. He adored my kids and would get me when they woke up when they were infants. We all adored him. My daughter was allergic so we knew we couldn't get another cat when he passed. Several years later, we were ready to get a dog. Since my daughter was allergic, we were careful to get a dog with hair and we went to several breeders to let the dog lick her to see if she would break out in hives. We finally settled on an English Springer Spaniel. We called him Jerry. As an ode to his namesake Jerry Springer. This was our first dog. He was easy to walk and play with until he started to become aggressive and after three years, we had to bring him back to our breeder. He felt so awful he gave us a dog he had that was older and very sweet. We took her home and pretty much fell in love. We named her Maggie. She is so sweet and mushy. You could cuddle on the couch with her, and she was funny because she didn't play with toys but loved to be showered with attention. The following year we added Chelsea; she was a golden retriever. She was adorable and Maggie adopted her. It was such fun for all of us to watch them develop together. They slept together and really loved each other. My kids loved them and took care of them. Later on Jade came to join our family, and although Maggie never fully accepted her, Chelsea loved her.

It seemed to happen all of a sudden, when we were on the way to the vet with Maggie Moo, our English Springer Spaniel. She was twelve and was taking medication for congestive heart failure. The vet told us she was deaf he asked us what we wanted to do. I remember thinking, *she is young*. He reminded us she was twelve. We took her home and couldn't believe she had gotten old; when did this happen? Jade, our Labrador, was just diagnosed with diabetes and was now blind. What was happening? I felt like I was running an animal hospital. The only one who seemed OK was Chelsea, our golden retriever. I trained Jade how to navigate our home with voice commands and if you didn't know you couldn't tell she was blind. As the weeks passed, Maggie became blind and it was getting clear she was confused, displayed signs of dementia, and had anxiety.

During this time I was so busy trying to extend their lives and ease their suffering that I forgot to look at how special their lives were to me. How having them in our family was a gift. So, I shared this thought with my kids and reminded myself to thank my dogs and tell them how special they were. Even as I write this, tears come to my eyes. I still grieve the loss of their love and the beauty of who they were. They were a part of my family. We speak about them always and I feel connected to their spirit. I was the lucky one to have them in my life. Each time I remember them I am bathed in love they gave so effortlessly. For a long time I could not even think of getting another dog. I am ready now and open to inviting a furry friend into my home. Before my dogs died, I never understood how people felt they could not go through losing another pet. I see now what a harsh judgment that was. The truth is any loss from our families where love and connection were cultivated is woven into the fabric of who we are. When the loss occurs the pain is so visceral. Who would want to experience that again? However, if we protect ourselves from that pain, we also forgo the opportunity of connection and love. I choose love. There can never be enough love to share.

A Message for You

It seems that there are times in our lives when the fires burn. It feels as if everything we hold precious gets destroyed. Our foundation is off kilter. We question the very fabric of what we know to be true. When you are in a state of urgency take one moment at a time. Do not think forward. Be in the moment, see friends, receive. Sense everything that surrounds you. It will allow the information to touch you; it will enable you to feel grounded. Remember: *Be in a place of receiving.* Let others in to help you. It may seem strange to have others see you in your pain but being in a place of healing and allowing others to give you compassion will allow you the space to just be. Many people think this is selfish to take assistance from others because grief isn't neat and does not last for five days. This is your logical mind speaking. True friends and family will put no time limit on compassion.

CHANNEL

Ah little one, do not shy away from the memories
that will show you love and abundance.
Create new ones beside the old ones that were created
with those that you lost.
Memories allow you to relive your experiences where love was exchanged

Bring those memories clear into your mind
They allow you to resonate with all that was given to you
in another timeline, another space
Those gifts are yours when you reflect back and relive the moments
Those moments of clarity and wisdom
Bring them forward into the now moment
[That] allows you to receive them as though they are new
The clarity that you have [gained when] looking back
at those moments allows you to receive them in a different way and
brings comfort to your heart

AFFIRMATION

Memories allow me to cherish the wisdom from
those who are no longer here; their words
come to me as a reminder

INSPIRATION

First trust yourself

16

WHEN WE HOLD ONTO BETRAYAL, ANGER, AND VICTIMHOOD, WE ARE BLOCKING OUR ABILITY TO RECEIVE.

I felt like I was in a situation I had no control over. In return I was defensive, angry, and always felt overwhelmed. I found that I was receiving judgment from everywhere in my life. It was a space that was familiar to me. I was so comfortable in this space, the limiting belief, the brunt of my own humor. The idea that I was the cause baffled my mind. How could it be so simple as just me stopping the chain? Let me tell you: it is not so simple. It is easier to look at everyone and pick on a flaw and then turn it inward and pick on me. When I stopped looking for it in others, I stopped attracting it.

I had this vision of what I wanted. I knew what I wanted to create. I could see the steps I had desired to take to create it. I always figured if I began my life with someone I loved I could create a home with love, respect, individuality, connection, and communication. I believed if I could find that in my partner then we were in the right place to create the life I daydreamed about it when I was younger.

When I was teenager and I felt powerless to change things in my life I thought I knew one thing for sure: I would do it differently than my dad and my stepmother, Gerda. I wanted to create a relationship with my family based on trust and honesty. I envisioned my home being a place where we could share without being judged. I didn't want to use food as a reward. What I did not factor in was how much of my energy I was willing to put in to achieve it. I didn't realize how much of me I let get caught up in day-to-day routines. Kevin and I would be a team to change the story I knew and create a new one.

We were living in Forest Hills. The park down the block was the meeting spot where all our friends would go. The kids played, moms chatted, and the dads got to chill and play. We all just got in and Kevin and I collapsed in the living room. Jason and Julie were ready for the next adventure, so I took out coloring books, crayons, and markers and turned on some video they liked. I was watching them sprawled out on the floor coloring in those oversized coloring books. Jason was coloring away, and I noticed Julie getting so frustrated that she couldn't stay in the lines. We told her it didn't matter but it mattered to her. The next week I went out and bought newspaper print paper. No more lines! I watched them color patterns and create designs that their imaginations invented. No lines, no mistakes. I knew they were both creative. I had a feeling letting go of the lines would be liberating but I couldn't see at that time how many lines I needed to let go of before I could begin to find my authenticity and trust my gut instinct with other things in my life.

I knew she was an artist, but she kept thinking he was the artist—but they're both. I wanted to be the witness to my children's individuality; they got to feel into what worked for them, and I got to provide the space for the creative I quickly realized Kevin was/is a workaholic. I say this with love because I adore him for his sense of commitment to what he does and that he loves his work. Over the past forty years I have also learned it meant I hated how it absorbed his time. I, on the other hand, just dug in more. I was as committed to our family and my career as much as I loved it and it fulfilled me, but it took a back seat. I can say I am so glad I had meals with my kids every night and as they got older, I still asked them to have meals together. Looking back I am glad we took the time to gather around the table. I would make these elaborate meals and get myself in a tizzy. Only to hear, "We're having chicken again" or "You could add more salt; it has no taste." These comments cut me to the quick at times and I would feel defeated. It got to the point I dreaded cooking. I felt defeated before I began. Kevin would see and hear how upset I was, so we began to go out. We discovered it allowed us time to relax and chat. I spoke to Kevin about why I didn't want to be always thinking about the meals and what to eat. Especially if they were going to be criticized. I didn't actually have to do it. I loved to cook but I didn't need a meal review each time I made something. It was easy to cook for Kevin. He was just happy he didn't need to think about it. I hear my kids say we bicker, but the truth is when we are alone it is easy.

I was really young when I got married. The truth was we got married young because I couldn't tell my dad I wanted to live with Kevin after we got engaged. I wanted to live with Kevin and be together. I knew it would make him upset if we lived together. I said let's just get married one year, more or less waiting didn't matter. We both wanted to move out of our homes. My friends thought I was crazy. I knew it was right. I wasn't nervous about being with Kevin. I remember walking down the aisle to him, seeing his eyes on me as I walked closer. I knew who he was. It felt like I was putting on my favorite slippers, comfortable, sure, dependable, and loving. My kids didn't know what we had between us. When we were together, there wasn't any PDA, maybe some handhold-ing. They would hear us dealing with the stress of the day-to-day things families do. Here is what I know: we had a loud home and we all had opinions and weren't afraid to share them. We were evolving as our kids grew and in the throes of it all things can get messy, imperfect, and even loud. Families stretch when they are searching for their identities and then seeking connection with each other. It is a process.

When we were home during quarantine, he got it every time I turned around, I was preparing or cleaning up from a meal. In between I was working. I shared how this responsibility was too much for me. We were all adults, and everyone needed to participate in this. So we changed things. I still get asked what's in the refrigerator when I am not even home. It takes time to change how things are done. I forgot to and would catch myself telling Kevin what's for lunch on a Saturday when I was going out for a while.

Before this realization, I somehow thought it was my job to provide cooked meals even when I was going away. I would cook like a crazy woman before I went away. Looking back on this, it seems so silly, but the issue wasn't about the food. I knew they would figure it out. I believe somewhere I was protecting who my father and mother saw me as. I took on the role and created part of my story around it. I tied my value in my life as being the person who made the meals and this by extension was my way of taking care of them. As I write these words, I am thinking I stepped back several decades and somehow stepped into the 1960s. I know what really happened was I misplaced my value and worth. Instead of just having the knowledge of who I was. I was in a constant state of overdoing it and claiming my territory. I was stressed to perform all the tasks I thought I needed to perform. I felt undervalued and underappreciated. It didn't dawn on me until I worked with a coach and began to understand my own intuitive gifts that I misplaced my value.

The next steps were tricky but thanks to taxi services and food delivery, things changed.

I was working with my coach on developing new strategies so I could use my energy where I chose instead of being in line at Whole Foods. I learned how to order my groceries online. I started to go to the city and let Kevin order for dinner. I went on retreats. I started to do things without asking but instead sharing what I needed or wanted to do. There was some pushback because I was changing the way I did everything. Including my need to ask. I felt like I had to check in with Kevin at every turn. It created many arguments between us. Finally one day I started to see I could make decisions without checking in. I did it all the time when it came to buying things; I always felt like I had to check-in. I don't do that anymore.

I started to listen to what I needed more and more. I spent more time doing things that interested me. I figured out a way to craft my days in a way that filled me up and if cooking dinner wasn't in the cards, it just wasn't. Here is the best part: no one cared! I had this notion I could change the situation and slowly I began to see I was holding onto an illusion. The magic was letting go of what I was stuck to and embracing what I wanted to do not what I felt obligated to do. I opened my mind to the possibility that things could be different. This is an example of one significant part of my life I shifted and there were many more.

When Jason was younger, he loved riding his big wheels hard. He would ride up the basketball ramp pick his feet up and soar down the ramp and crash into a building. His friends and he could do this for hours. The looks I got from other parents were full of judgment, but I knew he knew what he was doing. I trusted his instincts. So one day when Jason was four, he was riding his mini two-wheel bike and the training wheels broke. The man at the bicycle store advised us to teach him to ride his bike without training wheels. So, we went to the park and my husband ran beside him to get him started. I was nervous. Kevin said, "Go up with Julie; we will be up soon." About one hour later my husband came home and told me that Jason had done it. He told me that Jason told him to sit down and let him do it. So, Kevin sat down and painfully watched Jason fall and get back up. Finally he figured it out. Jason had this gut instinct that he could do it. Trusting in oneself is not taught but not controlling the situation and allowing him to listen to his gut instinct is something we as parents need to pay attention to. It is harder to step back and let someone find their own way than it is to pave the journey. He was so proud of himself. That feeling sets the tone to trust in your gut instinct.

Juicy Nuggets

To start any adventure of self-discovery you have to be willing to do the one thing that seems contradictory. That: to discover how to be more compassionate to ourselves. In order to start to peel away at the things in our lives that are no longer working we have to begin to learn how to receive love from ourselves. This comes in the way we speak to ourselves and how we gift ourselves the precious time we need to devote to what we desire. To discover or rediscover our value and remember that our value is simply being ourselves. That may sound like a flowery phrase. We all forget to look at what is right. What brings us joy. How to listen to our own voice.

The truth is we all have dinosaur eggs hidden and filled with judgments against ourselves and stories of how we wish things may have gone differently. When we have the courage to begin to crack those eggs, we need to be compassionate to ourselves and have the ability to receive wisdom. There is not one thing that happens in our lives that is not here to help us gain a new perspective and wisdom. The trick is to have enough for us and patience to slowly crack and chip away at those eggs.

Channel

*Is it possible to go so far within yourself
that time seems to evaporate
that you find yourself in the moment.
The purity of it feels
Like home.
Welcoming you and suggesting
you stay for a while.
Listening to your own thoughts, ideas, or
simply just breathing.
This practice is rejuvenating
yet we delay it.
Our ability to pause, stop, breathe*

It is met with comparison of what the world is doing.
The doing is what we think fortifies us.
What if it was the undoing
Merely being in acceptance
of ourselves in a moment of time.

AFFIRMATION

I have compassion and love for myself

INSPIRATION

Allow yourself to be compassionate for you

17

Marriage Goes in Cycles, Sometimes We Are in Sync, Sometimes Not So Much.

People get so frustrated when things are out of sorts that thinking is broken. The truth is one person can't create movement in a marriage; it takes two people who have a desire to create movement. The idea that you could be with a person for so many years and always be in sync is absurd. The romantic part of my brain believed that I would grow together with my husband, and we would share things together and move and expand at the same time. The truth is that we both had opportunities to grow and expand over the years in different areas. Sometimes one of us was growing emotionally while the other one was growing in business. We both were growing simultaneously, just in different ways. I felt lonely and afraid that I had lost the spark that first attracted me to him in our relationship. There was a time when I felt unseen and that I was not important. Looking back now I realize that had more to do with how I felt about myself. I will say that there needs to be one person in a relationship who blows the whistle when things are becoming stressed. Vacations and going out to dinner are nice but honestly it is the day-to-day communication and sharing that is the cement that holds relationships together.

I really can't stand when people say that you're in the immature part of your relationship when your relationship is new and the mature part of your relationship when you have been together for a long time as if the embers died. I have been married for a while and the one thing I can say for certain is you have to be willing to want more. I never am in the state of mind that we "had" a great relationship. I live in the present and therefore I am always looking to create time to connect and have more.

Even with the quarantine and having everyone working from home we have to make an effort to get out and take a drive, listen to music together and laugh. When you are living together for so long you forget to do the things that were once so special. Physical contact at one time was so effortless. Brushing your knees together when you're eating. Holding hands and watching TV. Now it seems we have to remind ourselves how those connections make you feel like a couple. We need to take the time to remember to say how we feel and share how we appreciate each other. It is to be expected that your life will be in and out of sync. When there is love and compassion, you can work together to get on the same cycle once again. It may seem difficult to create a new habit but if you give with your heart, you will receive back even more.

CHANNEL

There is a peace
in all of us
to be seen
to be revered
as something unique
special beautiful even sexy
to experience the energy
when two souls are connected spiritually
then able to speak through energy
shared connection.
It is a place where
there is a giving and receiving.
No one is more than another
there is a sense of completion

harmony and belonging.
When our heart experiences this
we crave it to sustain us.
This connection amplifies our frequency
any euphoria we feel is very real.
As a relationship progresses
the highs wane
They are replaced with day-to-day
Living
the original spark is there smoldering
it is planted deep within us.
Our hearts now
Are connected and with compassion
For ourselves
We can find the way back to
Spark the flame
The original embers are there
They cannot always burn fiercely
Love allows us to see the mirror
Of who we are in the people who we love
Can we see it with compassion
Can we see it and love our imperfect parts
Just as we accept
and love the imperfect parts
in the people we love.

SOMETHING TO CONSIDER

The more I understood myself the easier it was for me to look within myself. Instead of seeing all my faults I began to see my value. That attitude allowed me to also see what is good and even amazing right under my nose. The support I receive from my husband is a choice he makes every day. I could always be looking for something in a box with a bow or I could open my heart and receive and appreciate those things that no box could hold. I have been in a relationship for forty years and the twists and turns could not have been navigated if we both did not have respect, love, and compassion for each other. It is the thing that connects us even when we are feeling cranky and irritable. The truth is we need to have compassion for ourselves to be less than perfect. Realize that beyond our moments of feeling less than ideal we are with a person who can see beyond that and is able to love us through it. I needed to learn how to love myself through it and find connections that supported me to work out what was holding me back. I needed to stop looking at someone else to fix me. It had to come from inside of me. Once I started to appreciate my value and worth. I had more compassion for myself. I could give myself permission to not be perfect, to create boundaries with love for me, to create time for me. I began to notice what was in front of me all along. It is not always smooth sailing and many times I still feel frustrated wishing we had more time. I guess that is good after forty years. I am still looking to spend time together. I still have a desire to explore more in our relationship.

CHANNEL

In a place where acceptance lives
is the power to live your true self
Accepting and forgiving past mistakes
replacing it all with love
Love and its real form is acceptance
For a love does not allow you to only see the parts that are perfect
love cherishes the part that is hard for us to see in ourselves
the part that you are not proud of
no one could be empathetic or complete
without first knowing their own imperfections
If only to ourselves
each of us have to be imperfect

For the acceptance of all of us is the magic of love
Love for ourselves allows transforming what we view as Imperfect
When love is empowering it allows us a safe haven
to stretch ourselves and see all we can be
create a momentum to take makes us strive to do what we feared we could not
The fear of change is that we will not be able
to hold onto the imperfections
the idea of change is not to get rid of the parts that don't work
it is to change the parts that no longer serve us that are preventing us
from stepping into who we are meant to be
when we are accepting and cherishing those parts
that are less perfect
you are creating a space for magic to step in
notice how to love yourself fully
when we enter into a relationship
we offer up all of ourselves in the hopes that what is returned is acceptance
for all we are
in return we accept
all the imperfections from another
seeing for the trueness of who we are
It is this place where there is a giving and receiving.

AFFIRMATION

I can receive love

INSPIRATION

Manifest a dream

18

CHILDREN ARE NOT THE ACTUAL EXPRESSION OF HOW GOOD OR BAD WE ARE AS PARENTS.

We each have a destiny waiting to be activated.

All the romantic notions about being a parent have long since gone. My kids are now adults. The ridiculous idea that at some point I would be done being a parent is no longer something that I even mention. The reason is that I have realized that it is impossible to turn my mom card in. When it comes to being a mom there is no off switch. I could tell you I am not involved in the day-to-day decisions my kids make. The truth is we talk often, and we even have, like many families, a group message that we all share. I love that we are able to share all sorts of tidbits from a picture of what we are doing or a great meal we are having. We banter back and forth. I do not take credit for this. My daughter set it up and although there are days when there are sixty-two messages, I am desperately trying to silence my phone so I can work. I am truly thrilled that we are chatting.

There was a time when I believed that my children's actions had a direct implication as to how good I was as a parent. It caused a lot of stress and disharmony with my husband. I would say it now was a waste of energy. I was so concerned about how the world viewed me that I could not allow my kids to just be themselves. There were many times I had angst about the way my kids acted at the doctor or when we went out. I realized along the way that it was not what the rest of the world was thinking. I got this wisdom along the way. I can say that my husband and I were pretty clear that the direction they chose in college and in life had to please them. They had to live it. I can say we felt pretty strongly about this since both my husband and I are very passionate about what we believe and our careers. So, we wanted our kids to feel connected. So how did we accomplish this? We listened a lot and let them decide.

From the time my son was little he was adept at sports. My husband and son could be found at the beach after dinner getting out their gloves and finding an open space to throw a ball. My husband would come back showing off how red his palm was because Jason had a great pitching arm. I remember when he became the pitcher for his team. He was so proud. I also remember when he injured his arm and all the trips to the PT, we made so he could heal the injury. He trained very hard to be a pitcher in high school. He loved the challenge. I also remember the day he realized he was not going to make a college team and that he would continue to play recreationally. It seemed as though when he let go of this dream, he did not have another to take its place. He went to college trying to discover his dream and his passion like so many other people do. He was always a talented writer but never knew what to do with his gift. It was a few years after college when he tried several different jobs in advertising and writing. He decided he wanted to do something on his own. He was an out-of-the-box thinker.

He was excited again about what he could do in social media and analytics. We talked. I told him it would take about five years to be patient. He wanted to start working with people. So I said, "Who is your dream client?" and he shared who it was. I said, "Contact your dream client and three that are easier to connect with." I heard the feet bounding down the stairs and he screamed, "He said yes!" His dream client said yes! He is still working with this client and being paid for the work he is passionate about. I could have never dreamed this all for him. He could!

My daughter was always artistic. I spotted it when she was young. It grew with her as she got older. She took some after-school classes but basically, she was self-taught. She spent hours in high school teaching herself the adobe photoshop program and became proficient at it. She had a passion for it. She just never believed she was an artist. I knew I couldn't tell her this. I discovered there were portfolio reviews you could sign up for. So I signed her up. What I concealed from her was that she could be granted admission to the school based on her portfolio. I didn't want to create so much headspace for her considering that she was not an artist and didn't belong in an art school. We waited in line and all the people ahead of us were showing their portfolios. The professors asked a lot of questions about the work, but the professors were not impressed. It was my daughter's turn. I remembered stepping up with her because they wanted to speak to her. So I stood off to the side. I listened with awe at how she explained her work and answered the professors' questions eloquently and made some suggestions. Then she smiled up and said congratulations. My daughter blinked up at her. She didn't even think this was an option. That acceptance was such an acknowledgment. Her passion and talent were seen. She had a clearer vision of what she wanted to do.

Getting recognition from people who we consider to be at the top of their game is important. It enables us to see what we see in ourselves mirrored back to us by someone we respect. As much as we would like to rely on our own opinions and feelings, being acknowledged for what we do well lets us know we are seen.

CHANNEL

Hold tight to the belief
the notion that each of us
has the right to discover our true self
we cannot hand it to each other
like you would a treasure stone.
We need to have faith and trust
in them to discover who they are

the inner work needs to be done
to discover what drives us
Is revealed by living day to day
in the mundane activities of life
many of us feel as though
we stumble upon our gifts
having no memory
when the exact moment was when
we discovered our gift
It is gently placed within our soul
emerges when we are ready to see it.
Each of us discovering
coveting our gifts as the true treasures they are
It is free will that propels us forward to
Step into who we are with courage

AFFIRMATION

Let it go and trust

INSPIRATION

The essence of what brings you joy is your foundation

19

THE KEY TO COMMUNICATION IS LISTENING. THE TRUTH IS COMMUNICATION IS ABOUT CONNECTION.

I guess you say I am a professional communicator. The truth is I thought communication was about my ability to share what I was thinking. I was so wrong. Communication is being a vessel that can receive and then share what I heard.

So many times we hear only for an opportunity to then share our ego's point of view. It is as though the essence of communication has shifted. Has the definition of communication changed and has someone forgotten to tell me? I thought that communication was all about imparting and sharing ideas on a particular topic. So when communication happens between people someone shares or requests information and the listener then responds. Lately I feel the art of communication has changed. Now I am able to get volumes of information on social media. Media in fact is communication but to me it feels so different than when I can speak on the phone. My kids think this is antiquated. Why not text? The thing is when I hear someone's voice, I am also getting a read on their energy—vibe and I can sense how they are. When I speak to people on the phone, I can truly focus on the conversation, and it allows me to share. I find that this kind of conversation has the power to foster connection. The phone allows us to be vulnerable to sharing things that may be harder in person. It allows us to speak and be heard. When I am in a great conversation, I feel heard, understood, appreciated, and valued. People think communication is about talking. To me it is about the exchange.

When I began the process of connecting intuitively, one of the biggest lessons was not just my ability to share what I was asking for but to allow information to come to me. I wanted this connection, the effortless connection I could see my mentor had. I just didn't know how to get over the boundary I erected. I had to release the idea and that I couldn't do it. Instead I had to believe it was a possibility. What I didn't realize was I needed to trust the information I was receiving. I would always be asking myself if this was real.

I began to notice I did this in other places in my life. Second-guessing decisions or ideas. Allowing other people's ideas and desires to take precedence over my own. I began to see it. So, I consciously chose to stop asking to start believing in my decisions. At the start it created a lot of trepidation, uncertainty but I found the more decisions I made over simple things the more I built the muscle. The doubt began to ebb, and my wisdom and intuitive strength grew. Even today I need to remind myself to ask first before someone else. The conversation with yourself may seem one-sided and therefore not a conversation at all. The conversation we have in every moment with ourselves shapes the energy we carry and how the world sees us. It also changes the energy of who you attract in your life, both personally and professionally. Change the conversation with yourself; listen to what you're saying to yourself and how it changes the way you see yourself and what you are projecting.

MAKE IT YOUR OWN

Choose to notice. This may seem small (inconsequential), but it is by far one of the greatest things you can do. Notice how you speak to yourself? When do you withdraw or become triggered? How do you allow others to speak to you? Are you a good listener or are you just eager to share your point of view? Do you find that you second-guess yourself? Change the conversation by starting with something small and making a choice without seeking approval that is for you only. See how it feels in your body to believe in yourself. It starts with one choice at a time. Listen to you.

CHANNEL

In truth there is a place of freedom
where we can claim time and space
what do you need know, little one?
Acceptance
there is no particular place l where magic exists
it-is not a place
it is awareness of what can be
it is potential of what is possible
Where faith resides
faith is belief
what is the Hope
It is not a definitive feeling
it emerges from doubt
Hope is deceiving it feels like positive energy
Until you consider
You are holding energy for
Failure
When energy is stagnant
there is no use of power
The power to be more than what you see
in a moment we are challenged to dare to dream
Dream of a reality that is in the future
possibility is
where you are putting your faith and trust
into what you believe
The energy of love is part of that dream

it is a powerful energy that is beyond rationality and explanation
is faith in another
faith in yourself
it is when the ego is still in the face of believing
what we can hold but only feel
It is when you have acceptance
for the ideas and notions of what you desire in the future
without it being placed in your hand
to be in a place of love and light and faith
It is seeking light
when you create the space where life dwells
the desires of what you envision for your life
will rain upon you
for the love that you have for yourself
the trust and faith create an energy
that sways and attracts the momentum
that with you can dream into fruition and reality

AFFIRMATION

I am a good receiver

INSPIRATION

Choose everyday

20

Hold Every Event as Though It Was Designed Just for You

Every event that happens is a gift sent to you.

Who are we if we do not listen to our own consciousness? We become the things that travel around in our minds, all the judges and the voices from the people who came in our path along the way. Only we really know what our greatest gifts are. But the trick is to believe that they are real. If the only things that were real were the things that you could put your fingers on, then love wouldn't exist, faith wouldn't exist, and magic wouldn't be. I know in my heart that everything that is worthwhile and important is things that you can't actually put your hands on. I anchor into the feeling that those truths are in fact just as real. I keep my faith high and let the voices of doubt fade away. In my quiet moments, I allow those voices to come into my mind and replace self-doubt with what I know to be true.

So what do I do when I'm in a situation that is triggering? I've learned that I have to reach out to those people who are inspired and seek inspiration as I do. They remind me of all the things that I need to do to plug in to what I know to be true. I need to quiet my head from all the voices that rise up that contain doubt and judgments. All those voices I heard so many times told me who I should be and what I can and can't do. It's funny, when I finally got to a place in my life where I could choose for myself, all those voices slammed into my mind with every new action forward. I tried to shield myself from these voices in my mind otherwise known as my ego. I continued to offer compassion to my vulnerable heart reassuring it that the voices were wrong. In my heart, I would breathe in light and love and say, "You can't see me; you don't understand who I can be." These are the messages I would hear in my mind while showering, walking, and eating. These voices would surface unexpectedly, and many times would repeat messages to me. I never knew what I did that invited the voice in and I didn't know how to make it stop. I remember one time being on a date and we went to his car and parked at this quiet spot. The guy I was with was so cute. As he leaned over me, I could smell the spicy buffalo wings and beers we had just had. We were making out in the car and the windows were getting foggy and out of nowhere the voice came into my head. It was talking to me while I was trying to focus on his lips and hands. I couldn't pay attention completely to this guy and eventually he thought I wasn't interested. I had to cover and say I was cold. It was -25 degrees. I found myself distracted and not really understanding what was happening. It didn't happen often but whenever it did, it made me feel off-balance and confused.

It seems that whenever I am going to take on a new endeavor or take some heartfelt risk, those voices come flooding back. I learned that I need to look at the fear with new eyes. I began to surmise that those fears were my teachers. They show me where I need to stop and look at what I am feeling and take a chance despite the fear I feel and believe in myself. That sinking feeling in my belly actually means that this action is a leap into growth. I will share that the key for me was to have support from like-minded friends and my own coach. Taking these steps is slow and having the continued support allows you to take small steps forward. This is the part that happens very slowly.

There is no way to move forward without letting go of the old perceptions and seeing them as a door to walk through to gain new wisdom.

In the past when I got an idea, I would test it out by sharing it with people to see how it was received. Many times I wouldn't even share it was my idea because I thought it was protecting myself from embarrassment. Unfortunately when the idea I had was well received I also wasn't able to receive any acknowledgments for the new idea. I get new ideas all the time. I learned that now the idea has to resonate with me first. I resist telling everyone because I first need to believe in the idea. I spent too much time in the past looking for approval outside of myself. I need the validation to come from within. Then once it aligns with me, I can ask for wisdom from others. I am a personal growth junkie and will always be looking for a little more stretch, a little more insight. It is what I live for.

Make It Your Own

How can we move forward when we are in fear of failing? How do we try new things when we have doubts? Can we gain clarity if we are emotionally depleted? How can we shift our perception and see a challenge as a positive thing?

We have to make the choice to choose every moment. This process of growing and shifting can create a feeling that we want to escape. It is normal. Our ego seeks predictability for things to stay status quo. That is when we feel the tightness in our gut, and we feel uncertain. This is when you need to take a leap of faith and take a chance on yourself. Big steps need to have fear attached; that is your cue that it is a stretch. So many coaches I have worked with have said to me, "If you are feeling fear, tune in to your gut to see where you feel the stretch." Reach out for support to see if you can chunk down this idea. Make it attainable. Take stock of who can support you. I have found that getting a colleague to be your accountability partner is amazing. Let go of the judgment you have on yourself for having a bumpy ride. Where there are bumps there is wisdom.

Make time for yourself so that you nourish yourself. Self-care is not selfish. I know you have seen this before. Gift yourself with compassion for loving who you are. Holding onto the idea that everything is happening for you not to you. Compassion starts with how you feel about yourself. Creating that relationship with yourself allows you to receive love. Keep yourself in balance in mind and body and spirit always.

CHANNEL

It is a place for acceptance
lives the power to be and live your true self
forgive passing mistakes errors and replace it with love
love in its real forms is acceptance
For love does not have limits
(It) allows you to cherish all parts of your person not the parts that are
easy love
(It) is cherishing the parts that are hard
The parts that you are not proud of
without those parts no one could be empathic
or complete each other as being in perfect
being perfect makes us say and strive to learn more and change
The fear of change is that we will not be able to hold onto our imperfect-
ness
the idea of change is not to get rid of all the parts that don't work
or to keep the parts that do that service
it is to change the parts that no longer serve us and keep us stuck
they are protecting us from pain
stepping into who you are meant to be
means that you are
accepting and cherishing the parts
that are not perfect

AFFIRMATION

I am able to surround myself with people who support me

INSPIRATION

Anchor into your value

21

No One Knows Me Like I Do. I Also Realized I Need to Do It for Me.

The friends who have known me through the years have added so much to my life. I truly love them as if they were my family. I have a real sense of comfort knowing they are there and trusting the unmistakable bond we all have had over the years. When I started to step into and embrace my psychic abilities, I had so much fear that I would be rejected. I thought my friends would need time to catch up to the new version of me. The truth is it was me that held judgment. I couldn't share my gifts because I didn't believe in myself. (I convinced myself that they preferred the old version of me better. I bought into the old story that I would be left behind, ostracized, and not part of the group.)

When I looked at my resistance, I realized that I needed to create space in my heart to trust in my wisdom. I needed to stop seeking validation for who I was from others. The person who needed to create space in their heart for my gifts was me. It is gratifying to hear clients tell me how spot-on I was, but I still needed to trust in my value. I needed to see who I was, to acknowledge that I had worth and that all of it was part of who I was. One day I was working with my coach, and she asked me who I would have to become to feel like I was enough? What did I need to experience to believe in myself.? I realized that although I had peeled back some of my limiting beliefs, I was still focused on proving who I was to myself. It was so interesting as soon I shifted my perspective and began to see all the things I was already. My clients changed and I began to have a better understanding of how important it is to not only trust yourself and have faith but to believe that I had value and worth. This was a huge shift for me. I began to pivot my conversations with my clients as I began to understand that everyone needed to have a relationship with who they were. I needed to depend on my opinions and views as having worth. It was OK for me to say no; it was OK for other people to disagree. It was OK for each person not to want to listen to what I was saying. Actually the bolder I was with how I spoke the more I would discover who was interested.

I had a desire to accept myself and see my value. To accept anyone who referred to themselves as intuitive in general. I spoke to coaches, mentors, and coaching friends about declaring my gifts. I felt so odd declaring this part of myself. It was as though I was changing how I defined myself. I was truly claiming ownership of all parts myself. The truth was I wanted to be seen for all my parts not just the intuitive parts The eyes that needed to acknowledge and appreciate me—were in fact me.

The people with the neon signs, the individuals who offered services with an 800 number. I had this feeling that so many had a reputation for being inauthentic. I didn't want people to think that of me.

I realized everyone connected with what they needed. Some people need to go to psychics at a fair; some need a professional setting. Not one is better or worse for the choice. Each person attracts the information they need to hear and the person they can trust. I embraced my gifts and began to feel the uniqueness. My immediate family didn't resonate with the idea that I could be psychic. They were skeptical in general when people shared they had this skill.

It seemed like I was always fighting against this battle that I needed to receive an acknowledgment from them before I could claim it for myself. It was as though coming to terms with my intuitive abilities was something I was learning to claim was one hurdle and the next was to be accepted and acknowledged by the people who knew me. I tried several times to share what I was feeling and what I was thinking when I was experiencing it with my family, but they were very skeptical, and it felt like a lack of trust in me. The irony was that they were the mirror of what I needed to do for myself. After further reflection I realized they weren't in the work to explore what was unseen. They were unfamiliar with trusting what is intangible. Yet I kept on trying to get them to acknowledge the skills that I possessed. The interesting thing was that my immediate family and my brother, my father and my sister readily accepted this almost as if they knew it already. I began to tell my dad, sister, and brother. To their credit they sort of smiled and just asked how long I had known. My brother asked me questions and found it all intriguing. I told him that feathers are messages from Angels and spirits. I shared with him how different colored feathers had different meanings. As soon as I told him he saw feathers everywhere. He kept receiving messages. My sister just accepted and believed it. I had shared with her over the years some of the things that had happened.

I never mentioned it to my dad. My brother one day shared with my dad that I was intuitive. My dad surprised me and wanted to know how it all worked. He was so eager to hear as much information as I could give. He wanted to know how I got the information. How it feels. He asked me to share information whenever I received anything. The interesting thing was I spoke more to my dad about spirituality than anyone else in my family. I shared information about his grandmother and his sisters. Those conversations lead to him sharing about his mother and grandmother. I learned so much. We created this bridge for us to learn more about each other. I was so thirsty for any information about his grandmother and mother. They had been speaking to me for years. I knew so little about them. He was delighted to know they were connecting with me. He was so happy to know that it was all possible. I would share information about my stepmother when I got it. My dad's belief in me was the greatest gift. I never expected him to just trust what

I was saying. Thinking back now he passed away on July 19, 2021. I always thought he was a man who based so much of his life on the facts. One day when I came over to see him. It was dark in the house and quiet. He sat in the dining room on a chair with a cushion that helped his back, and his feet were propped up on a very old stool my brother made years ago out of some old carpet and some wood. I sat next to him and leaned in and kissed him on his cheek. He was always shaven with a button-down shirt and a sweater on and a faint smell of cologne. He was inquiring about Kevin and asking about how he was. Then, like he always did he asked about Jason and Julie. He did this every time I went. He was sad because an old friend was very ill. We started to talk about faith, and I reminded him of something he had told me when I was little. He said, "When you have faith, you cannot ask how you just believe that it is faith." I reminded him when he told me this and he nodded his head and said, "Yes, yes," and I held his hand. It came to me at that moment how he had intuition too.

I finally asked him the question on my mind for as long as I could remember. "How did you know to place an ad in the Austrian Paper for a position for a Nanny after my mother passed away in 1963?"

He said, "When there is no more road you need to think of a new one to travel, that is surviving." I remarked that he was an out-of-the-box thinker. He said, "I learned how to draw boxes with no pencil or pen; in Shanghai it is survival."

I said, "Dad, you knew you trusted in yourself so many times in your life. You didn't even realize it."

He said, "I needed to believe that there would be an answer and so I found another question to find a different solution."

I always knew my dad was very smart, and I was intimated so much of my life to speak with him. I am beyond grateful I had this time to get to speak with him. There were many years I couldn't talk with him without my feelings getting hurt. I worked on resolving it. Our visits always started off with me sitting in my car and setting an intention that we would have a good visit. They were not always like the one I described. There were many times he was unsettled or times I came by that he was too tired. Many times I left frustrated and sad, but I kept going back. It was too important.

He was the one who told me in our talks what made him think.

In the end his trust in me allowed him to trust himself. To know what he needed to do was right for him. On the last day we spoke together. He was in his wheelchair, shaven as usual with a button-down shirt on eating watermelon. He loved fruit. He didn't hear me come in. He was very hard of hearing at this point and almost blind. I slipped into a chair next to him and touched his hand. I told him it was me, Robin. He was happy he turned his face to me and placed a kiss on his cheek and patted his hand. He was pleased I was there. I looked at him this strong man and how now he was drooping over the table, and I just held his hand so glad that my being there offered him comfort. It offered so much healing for me as well. He was telling me he wanted to go home. How do I do it, he said. He was crying. He had enough. It was all too much.

So I took a breath and I said, "Remember the love, Dad. Remember the day you met my mother. How it felt when you held her hand. Remember Gerda my stepmother and how you and she enjoyed taking walks together and how you loved to travel." I reminded him of our dog, Rhoda. I encouraged him to remember all his friends, as so many of them had passed away. I reminded him of the parties he had and how they laughed together. "Remember it, Dad, the life you built. The love was in all the friendships and even in the arguments. Remember your sisters, your parents, and your grandparents. When you do, their energy and spirit lives in your memory." I put my hand next to his to let him feel my energy. I said, "Feel my energy, I feel yours. It is imprinted in my heart. I will forever recognize you. I am forever connected to you." We cried. I hugged him. I told him his spirit and mine will forever be connected. "I trust you, Dad; you are loved and perfect." He decided how to live and how he wanted to die. It is hard to watch someone lose their dignity and control. I learned that he actually gained more faith and trust in himself in those last days. I am so glad he did.

My friends that I've known pretty much my whole life had no clue that this was something that was going on for me and I decided that it was time for me to share this other part of myself with them so that I could feel like they truly knew who I was.

CHANNEL

The process in which you see truth changes
Your awareness goes inward
You have the keen sense of when the spirit is interweaving
You feel a loss of control
You are wrong
Control is your
You realize your truest version
Although it may seem like a foreign tongue
It is your native tongue
Familiar and yours
It is not something you need to learn; it is something you know
Reacquaint with the gift you already have.

AFFIRMATION

I celebrate who I am. I see my gifts

INSPIRATION

Nurture the dreamer

22

Just Being Ourselves
Is Enough.

Can we achieve what we desire if our daily thoughts have us believing we deserve less?

When my kids were younger, I decided to stay home for a while. I wanted to be the one who was there. I loved those moments as hectic as they were. Somehow despite them growing up I got stuck in this time warp of being the one responsible for dinner, laundry, and keeping the house clean. My husband was never a fan of asking the kids to do chores; instead he and I did them. I never stopped to think about it until I realized I was always living in stress. I was getting upset when someone didn't like my dinner or would complain they couldn't find their pants. Each complaint was like an insult to my personal being. Who was I? I couldn't see I had a choice. I didn't have to make the same choices every day. I could choose to do things in a new way, but I struggled. I was placing my value in all the things I did. My value as a person—my importance in my family had nothing to do with what I cooked or whether or not I picked my daughter up from the train station. But I couldn't see it. I was frustrated and believed I had no value and was underappreciated. These beliefs brought up so many inadequate feelings.

There was this inner voice I had ignored for a long time. I shut it down. I wouldn't let it surface. With support, I realized that I needed to release the judgments I was holding about my psychic gifts. I discovered my inner strengths and gifts, which I pushed away my whole life. I began to release those judgments slowly and created space to discover what my psychic gifts could be. I made a choice every day to be open to the possibility of what I was uncovering. I had no specific end goal of what I wanted to achieve. I woke up each day ready to explore what the universe offered. Acceptance of myself and embracing my gifts was the biggest hurdle. When I started to share, I began to see what my intuition could add to my life. The truth was the more I allowed myself to try new things, tarot reading, channeling, reading people's energy, and working with people to shift energy blocks I was able to believe and acknowledge who I was. The bolder I was in sharing who I was the more I attracted more authentic relationships in every part of my life. I finally recognized myself as being intuitive and I was proud to claim this gift. I could see that my natural inclination to use analogies to explain things and the ease I had with talking to people were my innate gifts and that I was meant to use them to help people uncover their innate gift of intuition and develop trust and faith in themselves.

Something to Consider

Our thoughts impact our daily lives. What we choose in every moment shapes the story of what kind of life we want to live.

If we believe that all of our actions increase our value well, we become the ones who always "*do.*"

If we believe our value is dependent upon validation, then what we *do* holds no value without validation.

We are a summation of the judgments we release and acceptance of everything that we are. In every moment of our lives we measure our actions based on the reaction of the people we are with. Our ego wants approval, acceptance, and love. So our reaction gets modified or even silenced in an effort to gain what we all want: love, safety and belonging. Seeing who we are authentically is not an effort in being vain; instead it is an important realization. When we can see who we are and know what gifts we are, and we can simply own them with no apologies. We can say this is who I am. Our egos step in and tell us not to because we were taught not to be vain or boastful. Anyone who is accomplished in what they do just simply states *here is who I am.* So, why is this so hard? It is because although our head knows it, fear keeps us stuck. *I need to recognize the fear and do it anyway. Create a new way of speaking about myself and a new story to share who I was.*

If we do not lay witness to who we are, we will always be seeking outside people to define what we are. When we are younger, we are trained to see our talents through the eyes of our parents and teachers. Later we begin to see them for ourselves.

CHANNEL

The fascination of what lies beneath is the truth you search
the key to uncover
what happy looks like
what if you were already there
what if you are living it
Would you recognize it
what if you possess it already
That is all within
What if there was nothing more to do
If we are fragments of possibility then it is possible that we already have
what we are searching for
Yet we merely have not uncovered it
if you reach for what you desire
Expand your heart open
what you know rises within you
stay still in the knowledge
that you know what you know
it is enough
It is perfect
use that to attract people
speak into what you know

All of the they's out there in the universe
want to hear speak more of what
You desire to explore
Concentrate on
what brings you joy
not what they want to find out

In loving yourself
you can be in all of this
there isn't more to learn just to discover of yourself
When ideas disseminate to people
they tend to hear what their ego needs to grasp
close your mind do not make things so complex
when you work at understanding
instead of allowing the understanding to bloom
you are using your energy
to figure out what someone else is thinking
Do not take on other people's feelings
think more of yours of your energy
What is the energy you want
what do you need to communicate
what you want to say as opposed to what you need to say
the message alters the essence of what you believe
the essence of what you believe is to be true
what people need to hear
the essence of what motivates you
can you see your value through it all
can you see your worth and value through
the message is being trapped within you
when you filter it with what other people need to hear
instead first always tap into your wisdom
share what you know first
what stirs your heart first
when you are doing that

you are acknowledging your worth, your value
all that you are to the universe
That's when the universe dances
as you reunite with the value in the worth
that you possessed
you possess in every moment moving forward

AFFIRMATION

I am valuable being me

INSPIRATION

A rainbow inspiration

23

You Don't Know Until You Know.

Would you expect anyone else to know how to do something before they even tried to do it?

I'm sure you've heard plenty of people tell you that once you make a mistake, you'll never make that one again. What they ought to say is that once you've experienced it and you know what the pitfalls are, and you know what to look out for the next time you attempt to do the same thing. How could you possibly know what the pitfalls are to something before you ever experience doing it? We all stand in judgment of ourselves all the time thinking that we should have all the answers to everything and then condemn ourselves when we don't. But how could we know?

Our egos are fragile and at times vulnerable and when the sharks come swimming to tell us we should have known better we believe them. How do we stop? We need to first know that it is OK not to know. Not knowing is even purposeful. If we allow it the information can come to us when we give up the idea that we need to have it figured out. We are not less or "stupid." We need to have a little more compassion for ourselves. When we don't know, we don't know. Yet.

I participated in online coaching courses for about five years and in that time, I went from technology phobic to a person who is able to see that when I give myself the time to ask for demonstrations all of a sudden, I can do a Zoom call. My friend and I would become frantic whenever there was some new thing to navigate on the computer. Who knows how to create a link, post a video, or create a course online? Not me. But *when desire meets openness, learning happens.* I still would not say I am an expert. But what I do know is I can find out how. That makes anything possible!

CHANNEL

Forgiveness

You have said you forgave
You have said you understood
You have said many things
But did you forgive yourself
Did you let go of all those
Feelings
Of blame
Shame
Mistrust
Worthiness
Loss of value
Have you let go of this
Where do you need to go
Within you
To let go
Maybe
The answer is
To
Love yourself
Accept
That the experiences
have you
It led you right here
It is your light
To see

To use as a beacon
To your
Soul
Find the connection to
You
Love all the parts
Especially
The parts you feel
Are not perfect
It is all in you
They are all you
Don't shut them out
Don't turn off your ability

AFFIRMATION

I am able to find out how

INSPIRATION

Step into your dream

24

THE UNIVERSE SENDS MESSAGES. LISTEN.

It was a typical Saturday morning. My daughter and I were going to the gym. We were walking casually juggling our coats and water bottle. We were going to the locker room to store things. I was fumbling around in my bag to put my ID away, when I noticed there were vendors. Normally, I just walked by, but one caught my eye. They were selling crystals, bracelets, and clothes. I began to peruse the bracelets and the woman shared that she had made them. We started to talk about the different crystals and the energy in them. I was intrigued by her I got very calming energy from her. I shared a little about who I was. She was equally interested in me. It was effortless that she was equally interested to hear about what I did. I tentatively shared that I was a coach and that I could sometimes connect to spirits. (I was freaking out speaking about this in a public place with my daughter right there—what was happening!) She listened and seemed happy that I was discovering this gift. She shared that she had a store nearby, so we agreed to meet in her store. I was beyond thrilled. I was looking for a venue to speak about how mindfulness leads to connection. I went to her store, which was so quaint and inviting. I explained how I felt about intuition and connection and asked her if I could rent her space to do a talk there. She suggested I come to her event to see if I align with her work. I was so thrilled to find her and bought the ticket at once. I was ecstatic for this opportunity to connect with people who were interested in intuition, coaching, and mindfulness. The closer I got to the event the more I was experiencing hot flashes, sleeplessness, agitation, tones in my ears, and hearing messages that came in single words or phrases. I was a mess. Right before I left for the event, I received a message in a voice that filtered into my mind and it said, "You will meet a white-haired woman with glitter. She will be your guide." I remember chuckling and thinking, *we shall see!* Then I closed my eyes and thought how ridiculous this was. My body was so electric with energy. I got there late and when I entered everyone was sitting in a circle with the lights dimmed. I quickly took a random seat. The energy in that room was palpable. I had never experienced anything like this. There was a person channeling in the room. I never saw this in person; it was captivating. I could feel the energy in the air and knew this event was going to be something I would never forget.

When the lights were turned on, an attractive woman with blond hair and beautiful glowy skin was walking toward me. She had peaceful energy about her, her smile was welcoming, and she said, "There is a spirit behind you with her fingers over her lips. Do you want to know what she is saying?" She asked me this question like someone might say, "Can you pass the bread?" at the dinner table. She wasn't excited or surprised. I turned to look her in the eyes. I nodded and said yes. I just knew it was my stepmother. The lady who approached me inquired if I wanted the message she had for me. I nodded my head. My stepmother had died three weeks before from Parkinson's disease. This message I knew was for my dad and my brother. This was the first time I spoke to Maria. She said my stepmother wanted me to tell my dad and brother that she was OK and safe. That she was not in pain anymore. She hoped that this message would allow them to stop worrying about her. After I thanked her, she told me she was doing readings if I wanted to sign up. I pretty much ran to book a fifteen-minute session with this woman. I knew she was filled with intuitive wisdom I needed to speak to her. When the event ended, I waited with my heart racing and ten thousand questions dancing in my head. I was so eager for my chance to speak with her. I had gone to mediums before, but I sensed she was very different.

When it was my turn and I tried to slow my steps down, I wanted to memorize it all. I remember putting my coat on the floor and taking several sips of water. I was jumping out of my skin with excitement. I sat down at her table with the velvet board and the cards neatly positioned in the corner. Then I looked up at her face and saw her eyes dancing with joy, big beautiful blue eyes. I glanced down and I noticed there was glitter all over her chest and she had white hair. I got goosebumps and a streak of heat shot up my back. This was the woman the voices told me I would meet. I felt a visceral shudder in my body, and I knew that she and I were meant to meet. I could sense that the next few moments were going to change my trajectory. I just didn't know how much. I had dreamed for so long I would meet someone who could explain things to me. Allow me to understand what was happening and give me the instruction manual to my soul's destiny. I knew she was here to give me answers and show me the way. My body was buzzing as I sat across from her, my heart was racing, and I could feel the swirl in and around my mind. I could see she had a glow about her. I could see light above her and illumination of purple, pink, and blue around her. I knew she was able to answer the questions I didn't even know I had yet. That was the day I met my friend and mentor, Maria.

She smiled and said, "They are yelling at me, so many messages all at once." She put her tarot cards down, looked up at me, and said the next words, which explained so much. She said, "You are an empath; you have many gifts; stop pushing them away." She gave me some practical things to do to stop the voices in my head. They just stopped that day. She explained why I wasn't sleeping and why I was always hot. It all made so much sense to me. The information was like finding the missing puzzle piece tucked in the cushion of the couch. The answers were so close all along that I just didn't know how to connect the dots. In such a short time I felt validated and acknowledged and I had an overwhelming sense of calm come over me. I knew I was on the cusp of discovering more, and I decided at that moment I was open to what I could discover. I didn't have a specific intention. My desire was to open my heart to discover all I could. I began to see her weekly for a few months. One day she said to me, "When are you going to stop denying who you are?" I was in such conflict; it was my big secret. My family and friends didn't know. Yet I connected each day even several times a day. I told only a few people.

It was a typical day running from one speech client to the next. I had signed up to be part of the coaching community. Every week we would have an opportunity to participate in a call with hundreds of coaches all over to hear how our mentors coached. To listen to what other coaches were experiencing hoping to unearth some inner wisdom and leave the call feeling more connected and inspired. So, this week I raised my hand to get coached on a call. I was so torn about how to share who I was with the world. I was a speech pathologist. Would all the people who knew me think I was unprofessional? What would people say? How do I move forward as a coach and respected therapist? I can share my secret. I pulled over in a parking lot to eat my lunch while I listened to the call every week. You never knew if you would get picked. I was eating my lunch and they called my name. I knew I had to share this situation that was preventing me from reaching the authenticity that I was craving. Maria had told me I needed to find the acknowledgment within myself. It felt so odd to accept this as a gift. I was coming to realize more and more that is what I needed to do. I was so scared to lose who I was. Now was my time to see I wanted to step into who I was meant to be. I shared it all! They helped me work through my battle and in the end, I realized I denied who I was to myself. I was shutting out the voices in my mind. I wasn't allowing my voice to share who I was. I had so much conflict in my mind and at the same time this unbelievable amount of joy. I needed to allow this joy to sift into my life. I needed to claim those thoughts and give them time and presence to be heard. I had to learn how to claim this as me. I will tell you it took me a long time to understand that this gift is not a cross to bear, no more than me having red hair; it just is me. I thought I would be judged and not accepted. People would dislike me. I have found the opposite. I have learned that the more authentic I am the more I unfold and attract people to work with. I have connected to so many people worldwide. Who are looking to uncover their connection? To uncover the gifts they have. They wanted to learn how to begin to listen. To trust their inner voice and learn to accept all their parts. To discover the magic thread that is their soul's calling and purpose. To discover what brings the inner joy, abundance and love I know that there is no end to this journey. The choice is ours to be in the work of self-discovery.

Sometime later I shared the news of my newfound abilities with my friends. I was going to see them together at a birthday party and so I packed my tarot cards in my cooler right next to the guacamole. The morning started with a bustle. In my mind I thought I would drop the information to them as if I were sharing that I was buying a new pair of shoes. I wanted to spit it out, hoping that there weren't too many questions. There were so many people there and we were eating and drinking cocktails like we always do. I knew I had to rip the Band-Aid off. I tossed it around in my mind. There was a lot going on. Food everywhere, dogs running in and out of the house. I was so scared of getting that awkward look in their eyes that conveys massive confusion. I started to come up with reasons why it wouldn't matter if I chose not to say anything. What did it matter? I knew I had to share this. I just couldn't sit there and eat. People were milling about holding beers and cocktails everyone was leaning in to give a quick peck on your cheek while simultaneously loading guac and deviled eggs on their plate. We were all catching up. There we were in the kitchen while everyone was passing the ketchup and the mustard and fixing their hotdogs and burgers. I just spit it out and waited. To my amazement no one said "boo." For a minute I thought they didn't hear me. Then one of my friends looked up and said, "Tarot? I would love you to pull a card, and that was it." They knew. Sigh.

I'd been so frozen by fear that I couldn't see past it to know that without accepting myself how could anyone else? I created the mirror of rejection to feel unaccepted until I realized it was an old story and I could hold up a new reflection in the mirror and receive acceptance and belonging. I then got how much I controlled the space in which I was dwelling. I knew my views and inner dialog had lots of power.

SOMETHING TO CONSIDER

I knew it was coming from somewhere, but I had no idea who was speaking to and also wasn't quite sure how to turn it on. Many times this voice would repeat the same message over and over. I didn't know how to turn it off. It scared me and intrigued me. I didn't think I was psychic because I thought that meant I was a medium. I knew I couldn't speak to people who had passed. I figured if I had that gift, I would speak to people who passed with whom I wanted to have a conversation. The truth was I didn't trust myself. I didn't believe that I could have that gift or that it was possible for me to be the person to connect with the people who I cared about that passed away. I went on the back for many years and was intrigued by the idea that people could do this, but I never trusted in the gift; I had to see what I could do. The voices that would come up in my mind came up more frequently and I began to share my experiences with my family because I was getting information from my mother-in-law and even my grandmother. My husband thought it was interesting that I was getting this information and didn't know what to make of it but he himself doesn't believe in this and so he was skeptical. I wasn't convinced that I had the ability to turn it on when I wanted to and so I thought it was just one of those things. It left me feeling inadequate and I wished that I could connect with people who already had the skill to inquire about if I was gifted. What I've learned since then is that you can have skill but if you truly don't believe in yourself and in your intuition and there aren't enough people in the world to speak to make you believe it. I learned that the belief first has to come to me. I had to learn how to trust my gifts and myself. I worked at this for a long time, and I began to trust myself more and more with each Tarot reading I did and each intuitive reading I provided. I started to see myself as the person who could, as the person who did, and I stopped needing validation that I was who I thought I was. I needed to accept myself and then the skeptic's voices became less loud.

Recently I sat in a restaurant we go to often and I asked our waiter how he was doing. He shared a story that had him upset. My husband listened and my daughter listened as I spoke to him. He shared he went to a medium and what they said. I asked if it was OK to share what I knew. I added more information and he blinked up at me and said how do you know this? I just said it is what I do. I am intuitive. He asked me for my card. He thanked us for taking the time to speak to him. My husband smiled. It was an organic conversation. My husband didn't feel uncomfortable, and my daughter went on telling my husband that people speak to me all the time. It occurred to me how things have changed so much. How I am so at ease and accepting and my family is accepting of me and supports me. I never thought I would get here.

So when you find yourself thinking and pondering over an idea, or working out how the new idea could take shape, remember this:

Ideas are the universe planting seeds of possibilities

It's up to us to turn the ones that fire us up into reality

When an idea does not formulate the way we envisioned, it is not because we are wrong it is because we have more to learn

The difference between thinking and doing is action

Clearing the fear that keeps you stuck creates momentum

25

Excuse Me, Self-Doubt. Move Over!

What is a story you hear and even hide behind when you cannot create what you desire?

Tell that voice, "Shhhh, I've got this!"

I put those stories on and wear them like a favorite outfit that is no longer in style, but you just can't seem to part with and give away, or like an old pair of slippers. Those stories accumulated over the years and became the way I show myself to the world. They encapsulate my feelings and experiences. In those stories I can't see how much I have grown and shifted. I see myself back in a time when I didn't know who I was. There was a portrait of me when I was nineteen in my dad's house. I felt like my hair was too short. I was wearing some rugby shirt that I threw on. I had no idea this portrait would take so long. I had to find the same head position and eye gaze each time and the excitement of having my portrait done wore off after the second sitting. I let my mind wander while he drew. I couldn't imagine that this picture would be hanging in the dining room for the next forty years. I remember when he showed it to me, I was disappointed. I looked so contrite. I thought that he would make me look beautiful. I felt like he captured me at my worst. My dad loved it; he said, "It looks like you with that faraway look in your eye, like you are dreaming of where you would like to be." I guess that part was true, I was dreaming about college and getting out of my house. I never loved it. I looked so angry and frustrated. It occurs to me now that what I was searching for was validation, looking for acknowledgment from someone to show me my value and worth. I looked for it in everything I did. I didn't have the wisdom that the secret to that was within me. I had career goals, but I didn't know how to begin to see my value and had a hard time believing in me. I had a notion of what I wanted and started to see the possibility of achieving what I wanted when I met Kevin. It is amazing what happens when you fall in love and allow yourself to trust someone with your dreams and plans. I remember sharing them with him in quiet moments and he just listened and believed that I as soon as I voiced the idea that it was already in motion. He believed. That was Kevin. He had my back. I could see him achieve his goals too. We had this unwavering trust that we could do what we desired.

That was the first time I dared to dream about what my future would look like. I began to see I had a choice as to how it would unfold. I began to let go of the stories I was clinging to from when I was younger and created a new story to describe who I was and where I wanted to go.

The story we use to tell people about who we are is like a snippet of the most important attributes of who we are. We use it as a way for people to get to know us. The problem is that many times those stories do not paint a true picture of who we are. I used my story to describe the accolades I collected but it didn't give them any information about who truly I was.

It wasn't until years later when I became a coach that I figured this out. I noticed I was hiding behind my story.

I introduced myself and said, "My name is Robin. I have been a speech pathologist for more than thirty years. I am married and have two children and a dog." That statement said nothing about me. I hid behind my accomplishments and shared nothing about who I was. I needed to be willing to share myself. This was one of those moments when I needed to see the underlying issue. For me it was developing more trust in what I believed and believing in my value and worth for just being me. I spent a great deal of time thinking about this. I realized that I had a hard time seeing my value and worth. I was so used to waiting to hear from others that I didn't know where to begin to discover inside of me.

I needed to take stock of what I thought about who I was. I needed to claim my gifts and have pride in them. Then I could begin to offer them to the world. Here is what I knew. I knew I was a good speaker, and it was easy for me to speak to people. I needed to see that my gift was not just a desire to help people. I felt compelled to ignite a spark within other people to see their gifts.

I wanted to share with people my mission. I was lost in how to convey my message. So, I began to think bigger. That is when the fear came. The bigger I thought about where my ideas could go, the more I became stuck and found I was not evolving and growing. I dove deeper with a lot of personal reflections and coaching and realized that all of us have the free will to choose what we want and if I wanted to achieve anything I had to release all the judgment I was holding against myself about my worth and value. I needed to hear the positive feedback I got from my clients and trust and faith in my intuition and call it my own. I was choosing to claim my gifts as a birthright and thank the universe for standing by me while I grew into seeing myself.

I searched to identify an adjective to describe my skills. There was this voice that kept needling me to claim what I did. So I got curious and conducted an investigation. I wanted to know what, in fact, makes a person an expert. After looking around and looking into the people I discovered that people who call themselves an expert simply claimed their gift or talent. All over the internet, everyone is an expert, then when you scratch the surface, I found people were experts at just about anything. The question I still had was would the title add anything to how my potential clients saw me? Did it make them feel more valuable? I tried it out for a while calling myself psychic. I discovered that the title was for others to identify with me. I would rather be referred to as an expert than call myself one. The confidence you have when sharing what you know is about your willingness to share. My ego doesn't need to get involved here. There was a time I would get quite jealous when someone referred to themselves as an expert. I learned a valuable lesson long ago from a mentor. When I am coaching, I share my intuition and coaching skills. It is like making lasagna for everyone to enjoy.

CHANNEL

Awareness comes from them from the heart
but it's the true heart it seeks limitless love, faith, trust
working hard is when we put our masks on
when we put our suit of armor on
to close out ourselves from being hurt and damaged
is it possible to walk amongst everyone
who's your heart too
Open and knowing
that the pain that you might need
Possibly so that your heart will accept even more information
into its walls and expand capacity
it hurts to love even deeper than it did before

AFFIRMATION

I dream with curiosity
I accept my gifts as part of me

INSPIRATION

Wisdom from pain

26

HOLDING ONTO FEAR CAN
BLIND YOU FROM REALITY

For as long as I could remember I knew my mom died when she was thirty-six. I watched my sister turn thirty-six and waited for her to call with a diagnosis of breast cancer. It never happened. Every time I go for a mammogram, I hold my breath a little and wait for the results. Will I need another biopsy, or am I good? I don't go consistently since it causes a lot of problems. Looking back, I wanted to have children earlier than my friends because I wanted the chance to create a family. I think somewhere in my mind I thought I could rewrite my experiences and have the relationship with my children I only dreamed of having with my mother. I loved being a mom and creating a family. It was hectic and crazy, yes to all of that, but it has brought me so much joy at the same time. I understood that the moment you begin to think about having children you start to plan how your life will look in the future. Nothing can prepare your mind to dream into the future once that new life comes. I dreamed of my son riding a bike, baking with me and swimming in the ocean with my husband and me. When my daughter came, I felt so much pressure to create this relationship I never had with my mom and at the same time being petrified that I wouldn't be there to share it. When my daughter turned three, I was all melancholy. I looked and delighted at her playing in her Tinkerbell shoes, and I couldn't imagine how heartbreaking it was for my mother to know she was dying and leave my sister and me behind. Looking at my daughter I knew I was laying the building blocks for who she was even if she couldn't remember any of it. I began to see how much of who I was because of everything my parents and my sister gave me. I was searching for evidence of this connection. I asked my dad again if he could find some pictures of my mom and me. He gave me a couple of new ones when I was two and I could see with body language and how comfortable I was. I could see our body language. We were posing at the side of our car in our bathing suits. She was leaning on the car, and I was standing in between her legs with my hand touching her thigh while holding my shovel. There is a feeling of ease and acceptance of who I was that bounces off the picture. In other pictures I noticed there is always some way that I am touching her coat, leg, or hand. The continuous connection children feel between their parents. The way they declare ownership and pride. What I also see is her expression, the ease in her smile and the joy she radiates at that moment. There is a picture taken three months before she died, and she looks so happy. I always wonder what she was thinking and feeling. I know what I wanted to give my children is all of those feelings. The ability to perceive love and genuinely know that they were cherished, and they could be themselves. I thought about this later on when my kids and I would fight, and I would cry to my husband and say why don't they see how lucky they are. I don't think they get it. He said they would never get how lucky they are; it is what they know. How true was that statement? Was I holding onto a fear of being forgotten, that all the little things I did as a parent would never be remembered? That is when I figured out that my children aren't my legacy. I can write my legacy and they get to write theirs. In truth I will never know what kind of relationship I would have had with my mother. I had such a fear that I was not enough. I wanted to rewrite my experiences and leave a lasting impression on my kids to be remembered. That fear was preventing me from living in the moments that were happening. I was already laying the foundation with my husband for who they would become. I knew it didn't come from a book I needed to read. Once again, I learned it was already inside me. When I let that fear go, I released so much stress and pressure I was holding onto. I realized it was already done.

OK, so I am going to get judgy now. I have an issue with people who go to the beach dressed to the nines. Come on, you know the ones I mean. Then they come down to the shoreline to take in the view and put their toes in the water. They are in their own personal bliss. The next moment, you can hear the laughter and bustle of children splashing, running, and generally having fun at the beach. The woman screeches about her hair and mascara and the children to stop running. Their mother comes running to apologize for her kids. Now I must admit I don't love getting drenched at the edge of the ocean when I just want to see the view but if I am going down to the edge of the ocean that is the risk I am taking. I know you are thinking, *what does this have to do with self-discovery*, right? Many of us, including me, like the idea of personal growth and learning about intuition but then we begin the journey, and it starts to get messy. I know many times I became impatient and even frustrated. The art of personal growth is that it continues to foster a deeper understanding of who we are. In our effort to accept who we are we also get to release those ideas that no longer serve us. We simply cannot do any of it without getting our feet wet.

CHANNEL

Create the vision of how your love can touch the souls you reach
The energy to reach them is not yours to manage or claim

It is their journey to create the space to discover their value
Waiting for the pinnacle moment when they can see the value of who they are
The time to claim to celebrate who they desire to be.
You can create The space is theirs to step into
Create a space for them to witness their greatness
To unfold what lies underneath

To release the soy
Release the fear
Release the judgment
To walk the steps you have walked to discover their innate authenticity

---

AFFIRMATION

My energy creates a legacy

INSPIRATION

How do we get unstuck?

27

THE WISDOM OF YOUR STORY IS WHAT DRAWS PEOPLE IN.

The more we try to be someone else, the less we are ourselves. When I started on this coaching journey, I thought I needed to tune into what people were discussing on social media. I believed I needed to pay attention to what was on everyone's minds. I thought I needed to research popular topics, trends in conversation. I thought if I knew this, I could direct my conversation to those topics. I believed this is how I would gain more followers and gain more clients. I thought having a topic was "trending" because I didn't value what I wanted to speak about. I believed having more people like my Instagram or Facebook lives meant I was on the right track. To attract clients and conversations. Here is what I didn't understand, what everyone else was thinking was less important than what I was thinking about. The question I needed to focus on was what I was *passionate* about. I turned this thought over in my mind. The more I pushed myself the more confused I became. It seemed with every move I made I had a fear I was going to lose people I wanted to connect to. I was so consumed with finding the big issue that tied everyone together. I wished the answer would just appear. Everyone has stuck points—this was mine. I was looking outside of myself to discover what lit me up. I was asking everyone around me what they thought, forgetting to tune inward and ask myself. One day in meditation I received a channeled message that reminded me that we all have things gifted to us in our journey in life. There are no accidents; all those situations that caused pain also brought wisdom.

These situations that happen are so we can gain wisdom and in time we can release the pain and benefit from the wisdom. This idea came to me one day from a channeled message. The more I began to think about it the more it made sense. This perspective is a gift in and of itself and needs to be shared. The notion that the wisdom we gain from our experiences is how we accumulate wisdom. The real work comes from discovering wisdom because it is interlaced with the pain. I knew that was a huge shift for me when I learned how to let go and release the pain of a situation. I began to change my conversation online, sharing how I shifted my perspective. Then just by doing this the people I attracted with this change in my energy were seeking a way to create a positive shift as well. The idea that these parts of our lives that were imperfect, that they caused distress and pain, are treasures. They provide us with the information we need to work through our emotions and let go of feelings that have us stuck in fear. Or events that occurred that we hold onto that made us feel unworthy, unloved, and unseen. These pain points cause so much heartache. They are here so we can shift our perspective about who we are and know that in fact we are valued, loved and precious. This idea came to me one day and although I believe it to be true, I get lost in the weeds still and forget this lesson. The truth is it is hard to shift my thinking from being unworthy to being worthy.

This idea that the nuggets I gathered in my life were the wisdom that I needed to be talking about seemed too simple. The people closest to me would tell me it is everything. I heard them but I was terrified. I was so resistant to the notion that all I needed to do was reveal what I knew. It all came back to acknowledging my value. I needed to really see myself and recognize my value. Once I started to dip my toes into the idea that I stopped asking everyone what they thought. I began to see I was already doing this in my coaching practice and in the advice I shared with parents in speech therapy. I began to see how much creativity and wisdom were interlaced in everything I did. I wavered between feeling like I wasn't enough and stepping up and stretching myself. I found that I would get all excited when I achieved something and then run scared.

I kept releasing the desire to compare myself looking at other people's styles, success, and approaches. I had to stop thinking I had to do things a particular way. I began feeling more comfortable investing in myself working with mentors who were able to encourage me to keep hold of the big dream. I started to notice I needed to go inside myself. To really hear and connect to my intuition and my guides to get the answers I needed. I found this process is not one you do on a Thursday between 2:00 and 5:00 p.m.; it is one you undertake and surrender to the notion that time does not matter. The trick was to surrender time. I needed to just be in a place to allow information to come to me for me. I was so glad I surrounded myself with people who are out the box thinkers. Women who are leaders demonstrated in their actions how to continue to move forward because they acted with passion and conviction. I started to see I was one of them. Their individual courage and insight allowed me to find the same in myself. I began to speak about what I knew and began to trust that if I found it compelling so would others. I just knew it had to hold meaning for me. I began to trust myself when I resisted linear strategies and instead listened to my desire to embrace variety and out-of-the-box thinking.

After years of feeling like I was ordinary, I realized I had gifts. I came to claim them one by one and was proud of myself. The limitations I created were stories I told myself.

SOMETHING TO CONSIDER

Having the ability and opportunity now to share my journey is a gift too. Sharing my story gives permission for someone else to take that leap of faith in themselves. To see and recognize their worth and value. What makes people stop and listen are the steps you took to change your life. Your magic isn't meant to look like someone else's.

CHANNEL

What is above the clouds the cloudy skies
Do they show so we can see what we can and create despite the cloudiness
Without the light
We hold the light within ourselves
That light shines bright
When we allow it to shine
When we seek its wisdom, we can shine as well

AFFIRMATION

I am connected to the divine

INSPIRATION

Less doing, more being

28

AUTHENTICITY: IT IS ALWAYS THE PERFECT TIME TO BE YOU.

Fear of being yourself can squash your ingenuity and brilliance. I used to want to quiet all the people who were my naysayers, the ones who always pointed out how difficult it would be for me to achieve what I wanted. My stepmother thought I should do office work and didn't think I had the ability to go to college. The professors in college who thought I couldn't get more than a C. The ones who couldn't see the future that I was seeing. Those voices were so loud there was no way to silence them. I later began to appreciate the volume of those voices because it allowed me to not become complacent and to continue and believe what I knew to be true. Without the naysayers, I don't think I would have had the unwavering determination I've had. I knew I had to prove them wrong. This may seem like a very immature approach in life but looking at it now, I feel like I had a kind of clarity. I knew that I was meant to do more even though my family didn't understand. Approaching every situation in an effort to prove someone wrong was acting in the space of lack. I was allowing my need to show the people in my life how valuable I was. This also caused me to be motivated by comparing myself to other people's success which in the end made me feel like I was always trying to catch up to their success. I worked harder to meet a place where I was earning more, achieving more, and that would mean I was valuable. In an effort to do this I was taking post-graduate classes to further my skills as a speech pathologist. In addition to my speech therapy practice I decided that I was going to hire a mentor and work with them to apply for a certification in my field. I made time to meet with her and write an in-depth study on a specific treatment I used for a year to gain this certification. I thought having this certification would make me more valuable and allow me to have more versatility in my work as a speech pathologist. I wouldn't be lying if I desired recognition and a certain amount of respect. In the end I didn't receive the certification. What happened next surprised me more. I was in a funk. Then, my friend who is a speech pathologist. She was my go-to when I was feeling overwhelmed with a client, stuck writing a report, my buddy who I go to conferences with. She said, "It doesn't matter, if you know what you know with or without the certification." I needed to see what I was doing already and stop waiting for the certification to feel like I had made it. Another trusted therapist told me she was glad I didn't get it because I already was a great therapist, and that paper won't change anything. That experience changed something in me. I realized the desire to be more than what I already was made no sense. I needed to start to acknowledge who I already was.

Juicy Nuggets

Things don't always get all tied up in a box with a bow. It is a journey to accept all my parts, even the ones that may not be so pretty. While I say this, I acknowledge that this journey is still continuing and ever evolving. Listening to people we respect to help us integrate ideas and create our own plans is vital. Allowing yourself to be part of a space where you can try out your new ideas in a safe environment with people who support you is critical to the evolution of creative thinking.

CHANNEL

Channeled message from Archangel Uriel
In a place where acceptance lives
Is the power to be and live your true self
Accepting and forgiving past mistakes
Replacing the energy with love
Love in its real form is acceptance
For love does not choose sides
It allows you to cherish all of a person
Not the parts that are easy
Love is cherishing the parts that are hard
Loving those parts of yourself that you are not proud of
Without those parts no one could be
Empathetic
The wholeness of each of us has to contain imperfection
For it is those imperfections
that allows us to gain the wisdom
Of how to learn to hold compassion
For ourselves

AFFIRMATION

Let my inner voice rise above the others

INSPIRATION

Wisdom is gained from pain

29

DISCOVER WHAT BRINGS YOU JOY… DO THAT!

Your job is to make time to do that as much as you can.

When my dad was blue, I told him to find something that brings him joy for five minutes. The reason is that I know that by doing that you raise your "happiness quotient" frequency. When you raise how you feel your whole body and mind look at things from a different perspective. Did you ever stop and recognize the little signs that happen in your body when you're happy? You feel more connected, lighter you get a sensation in your stomach. Things that normally annoy us slip away.

My dad usually says I am an optimist and that I don't understand him. That comment would frustrate me. Then I began to think and realized I couldn't understand. I am not ninety-six. I have not lived his life. So now I say, "You are right, Dad. I can't understand, but what if you tried for five minutes perhaps to find some joy. Reminding my dad in faith and that he deserves to be happy.

It is a funny thing I do when I am working with my clients. I ask them what brings them joy. It doesn't seem like a hard question and yet I think it is one of the hardest ones to answer.

I always find it interesting that anyone I meet can share what makes them annoyed or even frustrated. It seems most of us, myself included, never stopped to consider what brings us joy. I was in a class and the instructor asked this question, and the truth was I couldn't answer it. So I thought about it and realized that I had several things that brought me joy.

Real happiness to my core. It is such a pivotal realization and changes the way you look at things. I love being in connection with the universe. What brings me joy is when I use that gift to bring messages that bring a sense of clarity. I love being with my family and just letting the day unravel. I love to hear the banter of conversation between them. The comfort of being with people who I adore and wish them all the joys of life to come their way. I recently began to think that since everything is energy, we could tap into the energy of joy at any moment. I believe this is why I do some form of meditation. It brings me a space of tranquility and joy. I loved it for a while and then I could no longer connect to my higher self while doing it. I felt disconnected. I felt like I was missing something. I realized that this ritual of meditating for thirty minutes to an hour just didn't serve me. Initially I thought something was wrong with me. No shock that judgment and ego are coming back for an encore performance. They showed up to teach me that it was not that I was wrong or incapable; it was that I needed to find another way to find connection. It seems that I needed to find the connection to myself. I have since learned that connection to self can shift and it is not lost but that you merely have to be open to discover a new way to connect. I found I was no longer hearing voices, but I could read energy. I could shift the energy others felt. I also was discovering I could speak light language and initially I didn't understand it, but I began to feel into what the messages were. I just felt these changes and accepted them. I was grateful for them and what I have noticed is that they continue to emerge as I continue to grow. So be in the joy of your expansion.

JUICY NUGGETS

I love to have space to think, *puttering* time to create and be in flow. I love it when the house was quiet, and I could meander through the house or simply stare out the window. I depended on this time. It was my time to think and be creative. I missed it so much during quarantine.

The space to be in my own thoughts. I learned so much about myself and discovered my creativity. I began to see how much time I needed to toss ideas around and to give them space to come to their fruition. Gifting myself with this time allowed me to process my thoughts and problem-solve situations instead of always looking outside of myself for the expert. I discovered I began to appreciate my intuitive gifts. Being in the frequency of joy means that you are engaging in something that allows you to resonate with what joy means for you. It is a personal thing, and it looks different for each of us. Yet just like with ice cream or good music we know what works for us.

CHANNEL

All the steps that we take
don't always equal the pain that we have had.
It seems as if the pain
from each moment feels new, fresh
each time we think back on the moment.
our memories allow us to hold the pain
which allows the pain
to even feel so much greater
than in the actual moment.
Instead of reflecting
and holding onto the wisdom or our strength
in those moments
we hold the pain
For time has passed
we can no longer see any wisdom or greatness.
Who's to say that
wisdom cannot come from joy
Who's to say that wisdom cannot come from love
Who's to say that wisdom does not come from compassion
For It can
In truth wisdom is born

from the experiences that we are ashamed of
that we have cried over
that we would choose not to remember
those experiences lay deeper within our souls
with compassion and love
we can separate
the pain and are left with the wisdom
How could it be possible
that we were meant to experience the pain
wouldn't there be another way to learn that wisdom
The trueness of each event
is being able to separate the events that have transpired over time
And release that pain
hold onto the gift of our wisdom
our strength and resilience and see it as our teacher

AFFIRMATION

I choose to be joyful

INSPIRATION

Consider Magic – what is the energy of it?

30

CREATE THE SPACE YOU WANT TO LIVE IN; LET IT REFLECT YOU.

If you were to create the world you want, are you good enough to live in it? I decided to sneak home and see what was happening with the construction of my new kitchen. The kitchen I waited for more than twenty years. Each day I saw that dumpster getting more filled with all of the things I had in my house that I wanted to get rid of. As I drove down the long street, I saw it being hauled away! I shouted and screamed, so happy to be rid of all those things I accumulated, and I kept meaning to get rid of. I decided no more. Whatever I have in my home from now on will have meaning and something I love. I remember watching an Oprah show long ago and her words stuck in my head. Your home should rise up to meet you.

Let's go back a little. I had been living in a house with a broken kitchen for more years than I would like to admit. The last straw was when my oven broke. I decided that I was not replacing this until I could have what I wanted. So, the waiting game began. I cooked out of a toaster oven for about eight years. I made dinner every night. I would not compromise if I couldn't have the whole thing; I was living with what we had. I was ashamed I didn't have people over my house to entertain. I just set this intention that I was not investing in a quick fix. I wanted the whole kitchen redone. The drawers were broken, and the shelves were unsteady. This kitchen, the heart of my home, was broken; it needed to be redone. I had a vision of the kitchen being open and inviting, airy and welcoming. I tried to have people repair and paint different parts, but the truth was it was worn out. I remember opening the cabinet under the drawer and seeing sawdust from the drawer above it. I took a breath and just knew the solution would come. I just needed to be patient when the time would come. Our kids needed to get through college. There was always some reason that we could not invest in fixing the kitchen.

Many times I felt like, how could this be happening? I felt like I was living a lie. We were at a place where we could create our dream kitchen. Kevin and I were invested in this project together and we worked together to create this dream I had for our home. It took us over a year to get everything we needed. I was getting to my kitchen. I knew that before I could start the process, I had to declutter my house. I started with my stuff and then moved to every closet. Then we moved to the living room and got rid of broken furniture, old memorabilia, and things that simply had no meaning to us. My daughter and husband and I took turns throwing our stuff in the dumpster. The larger the heap in the dumpster was, the more excited I was about the start of a new beginning and creating the space. I remembered a day when I was watching Oprah, and she said, "Your home should rise up to meet you." For years I felt it wasn't. I felt it was barely breathing. I dreamed of having a home that welcomed me as I walked in each day.

Do you create the world you want or the world you believe you are good enough to live in?

I believed my family deserved to experience living in a house, getting a dog, having a safe play space in the backyard, and having a spot to barbecue. I knew we would have all of these things one day. It all happened eventually; however, the circumstances that allowed these things to happen aren't always what I would have chosen. I had a sense of clarity in my stomach. I knew it would happen. I would think about it often, but I believed it would happen. I never realized that by ripping out the old kitchen I theoretically began my journey of personal growth and expansion.

When I decided I would open up to my intuition, I accepted that it did exist.

So, I got the bulldozer out and began to work with several coaches. I learned many things, but the one thing I discovered was the more I uncovered and accepted, the more my abilities as a psychic grew. This phenomenon happened gradually, and no one was more surprised than me. It is daily work and recalibration when I am triggered or feeling blue. Learning to identify when a feeling is mine or someone else's and how to let go of things when they are mine.

The only way to acquire a new skill is to clear the clutter. I am sure I am not the first one to tell you this. Boy, did I need to clear clutter. All the baggage I held onto from when I was younger. The unresolved feelings of abandonment from when I was little. I needed to dig deep. I kept holding my mind and heart open to receive more. I never thought about what the end result would be or who I would become. I just was in this cycle of wanting to uncover and discover more about what I could learn. So this journey of becoming psychic was the beginning of me taking off the shield that I was protecting myself from allowing information in and also it was a way to learn how to handle and decipher the information that I was getting. I realized very quickly that I needed to trust myself. I needed to listen more and follow my instincts. For somebody who is always looking at everyone else to make sure I was doing the right thing, to make sure I was playing by the rules of the game, this was particularly hard. I still wanted to tell people I was intuitive, but at the same time it terrified me. What would people think of me, who would believe me, how could anybody take me seriously if I myself didn't believe in who I was? What I discovered was the more I believed in myself the more the universe provided me with information to let me know that I was on the right track. The more empowered I became, the more I believed that what I was actually hearing, seeing and feeling was real. Eventually

I started to share what I knew, and I started to accept my gift. When I had the courage to tell people that I was intuitive they were eager for me to provide information. I was so elated to be able to read cards and provide insights for them that they didn't consider. They provided me with so much supportive feedback and commented on how effortlessly I did this. The entire time my friend sat beside me while I shook inside, scared and excited all at the same time. I was doing it! I think back to those days and remember how I questioned myself and was afraid to lean into it to trust it.

I remember one particular session I had with my mentor. She said, "You've been given this gift from the universe. What do you think the universe would think about you just throwing these gifts away and not using them?" This sort of stopped me. I thought, *Oh, that wouldn't be good. It would be disappointing to the universe if they trusted these gifts with me and I just allowed them to flounder.* So, I practiced. I meditated every evening before he went to sleep. I grounded right next to my bed and said all the things that I thought I needed to say and that I rehearsed with my mentor about how to invite this energy and upper-level vibration. I did it every day. It was a ritual, and I wasn't really sure what was happening. I wasn't really sure if there were any changes that were coming about. Then one day, I was on the phone with someone I didn't know, a new client, and I listened to her voice, and I got all this information and I realized at that moment that I could actually read and perceive her voice energy and make statements about who she was and what her life was about based on the information I was getting from her voice. It was the first time that I did that, and I remember thinking, *Oh my goodness, look what I just did.* Despite the brief periods of excitement I still didn't believe that I could call upon it whenever I needed it. I thought it was a whim. Then after six months of seeing my mentor privately, I decided I was going to go to this class that she had with other people who were intuitive. I felt like I didn't fit in for the longest time and slowly, very slowly, I started to realize that they were like I was. I started to believe in my abilities. I began to trust in them and accepted that I could rely on them, and they were a part of me.

Juicy Nuggets

When we hold ourselves valuable, we create spaces that reflect how we want to live. Create a space that greets you; all you do reflects in everything you do. Hold yourself worthy and valuable. Believe in the gifts you have and claim them as yours with pride. Acceptance starts with us. No matter how many people tell you what they see in you it is you that needs to see it. I began to surround myself with people who are open-minded.

CHANNEL

Light from my mom

Hold on tight hold on tight
until you feel that you can let go
I will stand strong
I will stand still
for I know that you will go far
I can see it within you
I can feel the glow
the glow of your energy is large and bright
all the universe is there for you to know
hold on tight as much as you need to
let go when you can
for I will always stand tall
stand strong for you
until you know
see the light that's within you
where you have to go
do not fear the direction

do not think of where you are going
just allow your intuition
to guide you
know that I see it already done
I was the place where your seed started
the place where I began to grow
It was within me where your heartbeat began to spark
that gave you the strength to spread your wings
to grow
I have seen you stumble
I have seen you soar
I am no longer there
Yet I continue to be a light
in your mind your heart
I will continue to be a light
that shines from within you
Where the infinite dwell
Where timelines are no longer
And souls live in the light that is
that knows exactly where you need to go
but I stand back and I love you
Allowing you to discover
it allows you to discover
all that you can be
be the light for yourself first, my dear
be the light for all that you can be
create joy and happiness where you go
because it was a joy for me to have known you
when I was on earth
I watch you from afar and my energy is always around you
I am the love that always anchors you
my light shines through you
around you
know I'll be that for all time

that come to you be that light for those you have born
be that light and love to those that come to you
as I know you were meant to be
all my love always
your mom

AFFIRMATION

I claim my gifts

INSPIRATION

Truly you

31

WE RECREATE PLACES AND SITUATIONS THAT FEEL SAFE BECAUSE IT'S [THEY ARE] FAMILIAR.

When we are looking for external comfort, we are seeking a way to handle a situation and so we recreate situations and experiences that remind us of a time when we had just that.

For more years than I could count I would get a bag of chips, pretzels, and popcorn and binge on some show. That was how I put my brain on vacay. This was how I unwinded. It wasn't until a couple of years ago I realized that I began to look at this habit and how it began. The world was simple. I could just bury myself in some show and not think for a while as I savored something salty. Then I realized that I was avoiding confronting the feelings I had. Instead of thinking about how I felt and feeling all the emotions. I was stashing those feelings way down and escaping to a place where thinking was not needed. When I was young, I would find the hidden snacks my stepmother hid and bring them up to my room and eat them in secret when no one knew. I felt like a rebel, and it made me feel like I was taking my power back. I always felt so happy doing exactly what I wanted at the moment, with no judgment, no consequences. It was a pattern to avoid dealing with things I felt I had no power to change. I found that instead of crying over my situation, getting away from those feelings altogether allowed me to change how I felt in the moment.

I realized I was seeking comfort outside of myself to squash my unsettled feelings. I noticed that this pattern needed an upgrade. I had to rethink things and discover how to allow those feelings to have a voice and feel what was coming up instead of pushing them down and not listening to them.

I was used to taking on the extra things that came up in my family. The more there was to do the more I seemed to absorb it. I felt like a juggler who kept dropping all the balls. I was trying to work, be Mom, wife, dog mom, daughter, sister, and friend. I felt like my value came from what I could do, not who I was. I was unhappy, angry, moody, stressed out. Let's not forget about my need to control it all. I remember my husband shaking his head at how my every move brought about its own emotional onslaught. I wasn't happy. I woke up every day and prepared three to four meals and packed a cooler with food so I could eat in between clients. In those days as a speech pathologist, I saw children in their homes and in the office. My schedule was so tight I ate while I drove from one client to another. I took a lot of pride in what I did and loved my work. The work I did was stressful, and I needed to be present for each family I went to. I felt undervalued in what I did but I couldn't see a different way to exist. If you asked me if I were happy, I would chuckle and say, "I am tired." It was a popular phrase my colleagues said. Everyone was very busy and tired. I was resigned that there needed to be a trade-off between making money and doing something passion driven. I was convinced that if I wanted to make money it needed to be this way. It was suggested so many times to get help from Kevin. I did ask for help from time to time and he had his own set of things he did. I felt like every time I asked it came out as a complaint or anger. I couldn't even see another way. The idea that I could ask him to do the laundry or go food shopping seemed far worse when I thought about how he could do it "wrong" than just doing it myself. I spent the weekend jammed with errands thinking it was my chance to get ahead so the week would go smoother. We planned things to do but I always wanted to be home early on Sunday for fear I would be too tired on Monday morning. I always felt like the party pooper not wanting to go anywhere Sunday afternoon. Time would always get away from me. I was always late. I was notorious for having no ability to be timely. I would worry about waking up on Monday for work on Sunday morning. I had a hard time enjoying Sunday. Then one day I realized I was losing a whole day. After sitting and reflecting I began to find ways to do less. What is interesting was all the stress it caused within me to actually do less. I felt like if I weren't busy, I would lose my value. I still found myself making meals for my family if I left for the day. Telling them where things were in the refrigerator when I left the house. (OK, I still do that one). I did this even when I went with friends on vacation. I felt it was my job to make it easier for them. It was what I did. I started to see that by doing this I was teaching them to rely on me to provide it. As I began to see what I was doing I realized it wasn't easier for me to continue like this, it was not working. This story didn't make me feel cherished or valued. I began to shift things and allowed my family to make reservations, or order meals. If I didn't want to cook I did not. I stopped asking if I could meet a friend and instead shared I was going out. I gave myself permission to purchase things I wanted.

I also realized that I needed to allow the people in my life love and compassion, but I didn't need to fix it. I ultimately needed to hold them capable for being the fixer in their own life. To allow the situations that came to them to be the teachers they were meant to be. I started to see some shifts in myself. I felt supported by the people around me. I could provide an ear.

What I knew was I was stressed and losing the ability to be a juggler. I was comfortable putting myself on the back burner. My family never took the time to talk about all our feelings they somehow pushed on. Every comment that was made when I did something that they didn't like felt like I failed. It was easier to take the blame instead of sharing that I would not be held responsible or blamed when things didn't work out right. It was an old story that was not working for me. I could see it wasn't but wasn't sure how to create a new story. I knew to quiet my voice and needs and compartmentalize my emotions. It was easier to do it all until I exploded and then hated myself for losing it! Truth was that my easy, safe way of dealing with things wasn't working! I needed to find another way.

I realized I needed to control myself because of my fear, laced emotions, anxiety, and trepidation. I would get ahead of myself and live in anxiety and my ego had me dancing and spinning. It was as familiar to me as the soundtrack to an old movie. I knew it all too well. I had countless conversations with my friends, coaches and of course myself. When I saw it coming, I felt like I needed to run. It was exactly the place where I didn't belong. So terrified it was a slippery slope that would keep me stuck. So, when I got to that space, I would dread it. One day I was talking to a coach, and she asked, "What do you think this need to overextend yourself is teaching you?" My mouth fell open and I asked my guides to help me figure this out. Pretty much two hours later at 3:33 p.m. I was listening to a coach I love, and she said that when you are in the angst of moving forward you first get fearful. It reminded me of my kids. Whenever they were going to do something new, they would get clingy or melancholy. Then in a few days there was growth. I realized whenever we are working to move forward the old stories appear for us to reject so we can crush those timelines and create a new perspective. The old stories are not serving us any longer and the triggers from those stories serve as a reminder of the wisdom we gained. So when we get triggered, we have to acknowledge our growth and let the emotions our egos feel go. Bask in the wisdom we have gained.

Something to Consider

When you are working on something new the newness of it feels exciting, but your ego is on red alert as though you didn't ask if it was

OK. Whether you're speaking in front of an audience, doing a podcast, writing a book, or calling an old friend from long ago, your ego presses the emergency response button and creates this whole scenario that could be anything from feeling anxious to a full-blown panic attack.

The trick is to tell your ego you are just fine. You actually want this, and it should sit this one out. I know this may sound odd, but we need to talk to ourselves and remind ourselves that we actually want this. Create a new safe zone to be in.

CHANNEL

Light to who want(s) knowledge
Show them how to be pure
To who they are meant to be an answer for
You question
Ask less
Listen to your voice
Less speech
And be ready to lean into
What you know
Do not question what you know for sure
Allow your voice to rise
Be true
Know that is the knowledge of many that lead you to be
explain less
Be proud and true
See who you are and know
You are enough
Claim a spot of knowing
A knower does not know all but takes the knowledge when offered
Take what's offered to you
Blank souls do not hear
Do not try to catch something that wants no strings
Work less be joy

Embrace
What you believe and know to be true
Present in you brings peace to all close to your heart
The peace you search is only inside

AFFIRMATION

I am worthy
I can manifest my desires

INSPIRATION

Meditate to allow the possibilities to come to you

32

People Are Like Takeout Food; Accept People as They Are.

We are all made up of a bunch of ingredients. Have you ever stopped for take-out food at a simple take-out place in a strip mall? This is not the kind of restaurant with waiters and table service. You peek in the window and see something on the menu that interests you. If they could just make some minor adjustments, you could place your order. So you go into a small restaurant, the aroma is so good, your stomach starts grumbling. The line moves swiftly and you're excited to try something new. The people are friendly. Everyone seems to chit-chat with the owners. You can tell that the customers love the food. You get to the front of the line and say "Hi, Can I have the chicken special with no onions or cabbage and does your sauce contain MSG?" They look at you like you have ten heads and smile briskly and reply, "Sorry, we cannot make changes to our menu." So you leave, have no hard feelings, and find a place that has what you are looking for.

So why can't we do this with people? We meet people all the time socially and say in conversation I like them but…. If you're dating, the response is he is great but…. The thing is that people are just like those take-out food restaurants I just described. They come as they are. I spent a lot of time in my life thinking I could change people or change myself to fit what they needed. Both scenarios were not great! One left me feeling like I could never be myself. The other left me frustrated and judgmental. Along the way I came to the conclusion that people are what they show you. If you pay attention and listen and watch, you will discover who they are. You can try and dress your husband up but when he leaves to his own devices those jeans that are too big and old and that t-shirt you noticed has a stain are still his favorite things to wear. The question is, can you live with it? If you can't then you owe it to yourself to go. He is not changing. At work if you are confronted with a negative toxic person who puts you in a tailspin and takes you out of your flow or momentum. Perhaps have less 1:1 time with her because she is who she is. I think this is important to remember because I am who I am, too. I want to be with people who want to be with me, not their ideal of who I should be. In order to do that well we have to let others be who they are. It is a sobering thought when I think about how much time I wasted trying to adjust who I was to fit someone else's point of view. It only led me to judge everyone I encountered. I decided after years of unwittingly being the brunt of other people's judgment that I needed to stop this cycle. I didn't want to be that person. So, I took a step back and realized the only way to stop the circle of judgment was for me to stop judging others. I have to say that this was hard. I was so used to criticizing other people's outfits in passing or the way my daughter set the table. I just began to let go of the frustration and the hurt that accumulated over the years. I started to notice when I was with a person, and I felt good and excited to be with them. I noticed and started to let those people where I felt like I couldn't be myself drift apart. I feel like if we can't accept people for who they are in total then maybe we aren't meant to be spending time with them.

CHANNEL

In the spirit of friendship acceptance
It is not a place for bartering
Can acceptance of self be a commodity
Can it be something you trade
How much sacrifice does one need to take on
Before the realization of acceptance has no price

The story you tell yourself is
how you allow more into your life
The truth is it is all is there for you to hold
once you allow the notion that
You are worth it
Awareness comes from with them from the heart
but it is a true heart that seeks limitless love, faith, and trust
working hard is where we put our masks on
when we put our suit of armor on to close out ourselves from being hurt
and damaged
is it possible to walk amongst everyone
when your heart is open
knowing that the pain that you will experience
Is what we need to feel
To release the emotions we are holding
With tight fists
Protecting us from our fear of exposing who we really are
Oh but if we allow this emotion to be revealed
That is when we discover
that our hearts
will accept even more
We discover that the more we let go
The more we can be ourselves

AFFIRMATION

I am who I am

INSPIRATION

Judgement

33

I Am Bread:
Everyone Is the Summation
of All Their Parts.

We are not the flour, eggs, or salt; we are the mix of all the ingredients that makes bread.

I used to think that every part of me stood on its own. I was seeking my worth and in an effort to do so, I overlooked the essence that is me. I am not my hair or my voice. I am not my appearance or my ideas. I am all the parts mixed together. Once I began to see this, I realized that no part outshines another. All my parts work in harmony for me to be me. When I claimed one part as a representative of who I was, I felt disharmony. When we start to see that all of what we are is exactly the sum of us. We can start to feel when things are unbalanced that we feel misaligned. So when I am feeling like there is something unclear or perhaps I am experiencing negative emotions, I take a step within myself and ask if these feelings are mine. I have learned when I am with people I love, I can very easily absorb their emotions. Now, when I feel this and catch it, I ask myself, are these feelings mine? I am no longer in charge of fixing anyone. I didn't know I was doing this until I noticed that when I was with my husband. It seems so transparent to me even obvious but until I was aware of my empathic nature, I assumed everyone could do this. There is something else I have learned. We have the ability to hold the pain from those around us especially if we are empathic. Situations in your past that seem to cling to you still with lingering pain occur because you have not had the chance to examine all the feelings associated with that situation. Many times you weren't able to let go of the pain. See the wisdom you have gained from being in that situation.

I was reminded again that situations that create conflict are mirrors of the emotions swirling within me. I am in connection with people's situations in my life that allow me to discover the information I need to let go and release feelings from my life. I have that the common denominator in most of my conflicts is compassion and love. When I find my ego is on full alert. In an experience that is triggering it is because I am responding with defensiveness and allowing my ego to take the driver's seat. I catch myself in this predicament and I am always surprised. I thought I had resolved this. I thought I had moved past it. Yet here I am, all charged up. I used to think the answer was just don't get charged up, don't get so stressed out. The truth is where love and passion live, being invested in the outcome is part of the package for me anyway. I also realized that if I set myself up in a situation where I simply don't react well then, I am not being authentic. The new skill I have added is to forgive myself for the emotional outburst and figure out what triggered it. I ask my guides to share wisdom with me. I seek counsel from the universe and ask for acknowledgments in a way I would understand them. Mostly the biggest lesson is that I forgive myself for reacting and know that the reaction occurred because I am still learning. I also know that underneath the struggle within myself is wisdom. I need to remember to let go of the need to have an answer and a solution. That it will come.

This idea is a hard one to wrap your head around. How could a painful situation have any wisdom, right? All situations that come in our path are teachers.

We can also hold on to the pain, anxiety, or fear that belongs to your parents or even their parents. Once we begin to look at all of these things and accept them as possible then we can surrender to the idea that we can also let them go.

CHANNEL

What if I accepted the parts of me that are unsure
The parts I hold judgment
The part where confusion lives
If I accept that part
Take it under my wing
Then I can no longer feel ashamed
I can know that
There is more for me to unveil
There is a process of acceptance
If I accept the parts
I may be uncertain
I am claiming all of me
And surrender to the idea that I
Am
Open for
More to be revealed

AFFIRMATION

I accept all parts of me

INSPIRATION

Pain from wisdom

34

THERE ARE BAKERS AND
THERE ARE CHEFS.

We cannot change the essence of who we are, nor should we.

For as long as I can remember I knew I found I learned things differently. I am a multi-sensory learner. This means when I can see, hear, and touch it, I do better. I never could follow the directions in board games. I just flew by the seat of my pants. I always asked my friends to talk me through the game. I believed it was because I wasn't smart enough to follow the instruction manual. It seemed other things came so easily—science and history were effortless. I understood the concepts intuitively. Baking was a nightmare! All that measuring! I preferred to cook and if I could see how someone made a recipe, I was home free. If I ever had to read directions to put something together, I would toss the directions and instead look at the picture and figure it out.

I assembled a TV stand backward not once but twice simply because I believed I couldn't follow the directions. I never understood how people made sense of them. Others never understood how I could assemble something without directions. It never occurred to me that they relied on the directions as much as I avoided them. Flash forward thirty years and I started to notice how different people worked. How even my husband, who I believe is one of the smartest guys I have met, couldn't figure out directions. I realized it was the way we were wired. No matter what directions I'm given, something in me always wants to deviate. I'm an out-of-the-box thinker. This is how I operate. It is who I am.

So I got curious and noticed how some people gravitate to more free flow and some needed the organization of lists and charts. I made light of it but started to see that the more I trusted my intuition the more I feared concrete strategies and the more I had a desire to lean into my intuitive wisdom at the moment. When I felt like I was downloading information I began to surrender to it and trust the wisdom that I was receiving. I began to ask my guides questions and awaited their answers. I started to notice information everywhere. I began to see it and use those signs as signs from the universe to keep on trusting, asking and being open to receiving. It made me think of how chefs incorporate flavors and techniques to create their masterpieces. Bakers tend to stick with recipes and are very aligned with being precise. It is the precision that allows them to thrive.

Whether you are a chef or a baker, there is a process you follow, and your inherent intuition guides you there. The big shift comes when the chef adapts baker principles, and the baker adapts out-of-the-box thinking. When we borrow from the strength of where we are not comfortable, we allow ourselves to expand and grow.

I know that I am an out-of-the-box thinker. I tend to gravitate toward feeling my way through things rather than reading the black and white directions. It is who I am. No matter what directions I'm given, something in me always wants to deviate. I always knew this was how I operate.

Find the spaces in the quiet to hear your heartbeat. Let the sound soothe you. Take moments in your day to pause—to breathe—to just be. Investing time for you is an investment that multiplies in all you do. Giving the gift of time for yourself seems indulgent. Go ahead, indulge; you are worth it!

Juicy Nuggets

There are those who need precision and rules and need the parameters to make sense of the world. Then there are those who think out of the box. The people who cook with no recipe. They sprinkle and add what they feel they need. They create things in the moment. Both are beautiful. Which one are you? Simply acknowledging it will allow you to make peace with the very nature of you. It is not better to be one or the other. Simply observe who you are and see where you can expand by considering another perspective. Receiving is a funny thing. I wanted information but first I needed to do personal growth work. Focusing on upgrading how I valued who I was. Believing that I had worth. Trusting in myself. It is a process to be sure and in every step, I began to gain more of an understanding of trust and faith in myself. It started with a shift in how I valued myself.

CHANNEL

Put down the story you have learned
take a new perspective
It takes wisdom to know that there is more to gain
when seeing all sides of the story
Even if you think you have looked already
Look again
How can you see what your mind is not able to witness
In your life you encounter the story over and over
the reason is
you grow
in that growth your ability to reap information alters.
See the sides without your ego
Without worrying about judgment
With fear of not being accepted
See the story for the wisdom you can now see
Do not judge your inability to have not seen it sooner
It wasn't your time
Look at it anew
Take in the wisdom you can gain now that you have grown inside
To see. the wholeness of the story

See how without the story
You may not have grown
Made the choices you made
Now is the time to claim a new perspective
Use the energy to propel you into a new understanding
A new truth
A new appreciation of you

AFFIRMATION

I can trust myself

INSPIRATION

Reset

35

LOVE HOLDS INFINITE POSSIBILITIES.

Abundance shouldn't have limits.

I remember when I had my son. I didn't trust my own instincts. I thought I should ask and listen to experts. All the information that was coming to me from books, articles, and neighbors' suggestions was overwhelming. The comments were endless, and I heard them all. In those early days of motherhood I felt like I didn't know how. The more they told me to let my son cry, don't hold him so much and never felt right in my soul. All I knew was that when he was crying and when I held him close to me wrapped in my housecoat, he was content. I remember thinking how could holding a crying baby be detrimental. My instinct told me he was a baby. I remember talking about this to my mother-in-law about this. She said, "They are this little once," as if to say enjoy him don't worry. My mother-in-law Julia was such a wise woman; if you had told her this she would have argued and laughed. She became a mother late in her life. There was a time she thought that this dream would never happen. She was a Holocaust survivor. She did not speak of her experience, but it was easy to see how she chose to live. She doted on her children, and it gave her joy to do it. She told me many times to let go of having everything be perfect. Mess is what makes life. She said, "When things are too perfect it means there is no living happening." I anchored onto those words when I saw the toys disbursed in piles around my home, shoes and coats hanging on every surface around the apartment. I would take a breath and remember her words. When I got triggered by the clutter, I needed to remember that life was happening, and mess was just the outer result of it. Instead it was jumbled and messy. Her words allowed me to remember that a good life is one that has a mess. I will admit I cleaned up, exasperated at times at how quickly it became chaos again and again. Now, my kids are adults and there are no toys around my house. I still see clutter in my home and have to remind myself that clutter symbolizes living and that my house is lived in. Trying to control the outside usually means that I haven't taken the time to honor myself with the gift of time. I have learned over and over that if I am pushing to do too many things and I am not making time for me to breathe the usual result is inner turmoil. All of a sudden, every noise, dust bunny, and cup fill up my vision to the point I can't see anything else. I have a toolbox of things that I go to that help me regain my inner goddess. You may be thinking how taking time for myself will bring abundance and love. The thing is if we are always in a place of giving to everyone but not ourselves, we are always in action. When I began to surrender to the idea that I can and should receive. My relationship with how I saw myself shifted. I had to be willing to see myself as valuable as the people who I give to. When I began to take this on, I noticed I began receiving it in every area of my life.

Juicy Nuggets

What do you put in your toolbox? First of all it doesn't actually need to be a box you can hold. It is a box you can list. I have gathered things over the years, and I have everything in my box from a manicure to taking my shoes off and standing in the grass. How you cultivate yourself is making a point to notice what you do that feels good down to your soul. It is a space you can create where you feel connected and free of worry and the need to do anything. In my toolbox I have things that take moments like taking three clearing breaths, to taking a drive to the ocean. You know it is right for you when you are able to find serenity and connection to yourself. Many people feel they need to be in a space where their mind is quiet. I say let the voices come in. Let your mind go free. See what thoughts rise to the surface. Some of my best ideas are when I surrender to this practice. I have found that when I do this, I am giving myself to let my thinking brain rest for how much time. I am in a place to receive information. Over the years I have found that I can slip into this state of mind with greater ease. I also know that I am receiving information from my higher self. This connection feels so fundamental to how I operate now. In the beginning it was more purposeful. Being abundant is not a destination; it is a state of mind.

CHANNEL

Is it possible to go so far with yourself
that time seems to evaporate
that you find yourself in the moment.
The purity of it feels
Like home.
Welcoming you
suggesting you stay for a while.
Listening to your own thoughts, ideas, or simply just breathing.
This practice is rejuvenating
yet we delay it.
Our ability to
Pause, stop, breathe
is met with comparison of what the world is doing.
Doing what we think of it fortifies us.
What if it was the undoing?
Merely being in acceptance of ourselves in a moment of time.

AFFIRMATION

I have value I can receive

INSPIRATION

Abundance and love

36

DINNER CONVERSATIONS ARE THE KEY TO FAMILY CONNECTIONS.

It is what we do every day that builds connections.

It was next to impossible to have a meal with my husband when we started our family. It felt like we were on a timer. In mere seconds my son would complain and need to be held. We discovered early on that the best way to have alone time would be to pick up lunch and have a picnic in the car while my son slept in his car seat. It became our favorite pastime, going on long drives to put my son to sleep and finding a scenic spot where we could listen to music and eat in the car. It was so much fun to have these adventures. Three years later when my daughter was born, we tried to continue this strategy to create some time for us to be together, but it did not last for long. So we tried to go out at the start. It was a disaster. My son could never sit long enough to make past appetizers. I remember sitting alone on vacation while my husband played with my son outside. So we stopped for a while and ate at home. What I discovered was that when we sat at the table at home, he wanted to sit with us and try our food and play under our feet; he just wasn't able to sit. As they both grew as hectic as family dinners can be there is a richness in connection that develops when everyone is sitting at the table. Even through their teenage years when my son would have rather ordered take out every night, we still had family dinners. The conversations were stiff at times, but we kept having them anyway. I always felt dinner is where connections happen. Family dinners moved out of the house for a while since it gave us time to chat rather than cook and clean. It created a stress-free atmosphere. Everyone got what they wanted to eat, and we got to be together. We kept trying and eventually we came out on the other side of the teenage years. During college dinner was a quick touch base and we would talk about movies, music, travel. It became easier to go out and we somehow shifted into a group and started to all have a good time. There were times there was conflict but looking back I am glad they both felt they could learn how to air their feelings. The truth is our family is the playing ground for learning how to be in a group. How to share your feelings without hurting someone else. How to lean on people when you need it and how to ask for space. There were times I felt we would never be harmonious. I would dedicate my yoga every day to harmony in my family. One day I was doing yoga and when I thought about what I wanted to dedicate my practice to, I realized we had harmony. A big smile spread across my lips. I can tell you that my husband and I take such pride in our family; it means so much to us. They are what they are because of their unique ability to express who they are. We just kept on sticking with it. We accept each other even though there are things that make each of us nuts. The great thing is that we still come together. My husband says he feels like a rich man when he can go to dinner with his family. It brings him so much joy. Over the past few years we vacationed together, and it is some of my best memories. That getaway lunch my husband started thirty-three years ago has merged into so much more. We all have grown separately and together. The dynamics of my family are not so unique. I know there are millions of families who do this. I am reflecting on this because I realized how this was my husband's and my heart's desire to create a space of unity. It is a vision we hold in our hearts. You have to hold that vision with love and nurture it, have faith in it. You see the outcome in your mind the way you desire it. It is my experience that when it comes it is even better than you could have imagined.

JUICY NUGGETS

When we have a desire or a dream, we keep them to ourselves. We are afraid to voice it almost like if we say it out loud it will not happen. I have learned to write it down. I say it to myself and then I go a few steps further. I create a vision.

Here is how.

1. Find a comfortable chair.
2. Take five breaths, feel the air fill up your belly and then pay attention to the air leaving over your lips.
3. On the last breath find the connection to your intuition to your heart.
4. Think of a desire you have.
5. Create the entire vision:

Who is there?

What are you doing?

Where are you?

How do you feel?

Hold that feeling in your mind and heart.

6. Repeat these steps every so often to call in the energy and create the vision.

My vision I knew would take years to manifest. I created this vision whenever I did yoga. I have done this with other ideas even with this book. I have found it so helpful, and it allowed me to anchor into attracting the energy to create the outcome. When you trust in the fact that your ideas have energy and having faith in them creates a forward momentum then you can surrender time and just know it will come.

CHANNEL

Hold the energy in your heart, little one
Let the energy warm you and stir your desires
You are the one to call it in
Bring forth what you desire with your heart's desire
Nurture it with love and faith
When things are dismal
Start anew
Hold your vision close and
Allow it to wings to fly
Surrender to the intention
Have trust and faith that it will happen

AFFIRMATION

I can create my future

INSPIRATION

Fill Your Soul

37

THE OUT-OF-THE-BOX THINKER MAKES SENSE OF THE NUANCES IN THE WORLD.

If you learn by doing, then you know that experiences are your greatest teacher.

I spent quite some time priding my value based on what I learned from school and classes. If you think about how we learn traditionally it leaves little time for anyone to lean into what they *know* as opposed to what they have *learned.* There is wisdom in being an active observer. When we were young, we observed our parents, siblings, teachers, and friends. Most of the education system is based on being an observer. The thing is many of us need more we need to also be able to be active participants. I was one of those kids. I always did better if I could watch someone do it while they explained it. So you can imagine me and millions of other people really appreciated YouTube when it came around.

There are also people who learn in many different ways. The people who think of a new way to do a common task or a simple trick to fix a problem, those people see things with new eyes. When I took this road to develop my intuition, I quickly realized that how I began to notice things around me shifted. I saw the things around me as a way to receive information from the universe. Problems were happening for me, not "to me." It was my choice to see them as a message or an annoyance. This was not always easy to see because many situations that are painful and upsetting are difficult to see as a gift. The truth is all situations allow us to build our resilience and look back and know that we were able to persevere. The painful ones are harder to look at as gifts but those usually come with our greatest lessons. I always told my kids to take note of what they don't like but to make sure they pay attention to things they do naturally well. I always felt that you should start your direction in life with something that brought you joy.

CHANNEL

Be all you allow
Bring in compassion, love
See all that is
See all you create
Know it is your hand that mixes it up
Know that your gifts and beauty
allow for them all to open their hearts
Proclaim that which is within

AFFIRMATION

I can discover the wisdom

INSPIRATION

Acceptance

38

A Thought Is Just a Thought until You Put Your Voice Behind It.

Turn off the outside voices and just proceed. I heard voices in the quiet as if someone had turned on my own personal radio station in my head for so long. They taunted me more than soothed me. When I was quiet or while I was running, dancing, and even showering. I would dread it at times since I didn't know how to make them stop. I didn't share this with my family or friends. I wasn't sure what to say about it.

If I were engaged in a guided meditation I could focus on the guide's voice and block the voices in my head. I found these voices distracting and wished I knew more. It was usually a phrase but sometimes it was a thought or string of thoughts. When I had our first child, the voices became much louder. One day I was driving to see my friend for a play date. My son was safe in his car seat, and I heard a voice in my head clearly that said, "Move over" while I was driving in the middle lane of the highway. I glanced in my rearview mirror. I was grateful there was no traffic and swiftly changed lanes. We were safe. In the next moment I heard the sound that convinced me how connected I truly was. The car beside me braked suddenly and I realized that the car was out of control because a bunch of pennies had been thrown on its windshield. At that moment I knew two things: that the voice I heard was real and that it was looking out for me. I began to talk to have conversations hoping to bring the voice back, wishing it would come and share some wisdom. The voice came and went randomly. I wouldn't have the courage to understand who was speaking to me and how to connect to the voice for twenty-six years.

I eventually had the courage to share this with my husband and kids and they didn't make much of it. They passed it off as a daydream. In my gut I knew it was something greater. Yet, it was easier for me to do the same. It allowed me to hide my truth. It was easier to think it was a daydream. I didn't pursue it. I thought of it as a quirk, something weird. The messages, on the other hand, kept coming. I suspected it was something more, but I still didn't have the inclination to learn more. I pushed it away. I felt the need to convince my husband it was more, but it was just not something he was inclined to believe in. I was fascinated by all of it. I watched reality shows with mediums and loved every moment. I was intrigued by it all. I didn't identify with the idea of me being medium. I couldn't see or hear people whenever I desired. Then, one day I was at my sister's house. We were having a cup of tea. My sister knew I heard these voices. She asked me to hold a bracelet from a friend of hers. When I did, I got a stream of information. She was so surprised and excited, and I realized I was connecting to her friend's energy.

I was excited but didn't know how or what to do next but in the next moment I was getting information that this friend was not here anymore. There was information about a boat and that his daughter would be on it with her husband and baby. The other daughter was with someone too. My sister and others were on this boat. When I shared this information, she said, "Oh, he wants his ashes spread in six months when we have a celebration of life boat ride."

She didn't know but wasn't surprised that his daughter was pregnant. I was surprised that I could do this. Yet I still felt that I wasn't a medium. I had several events that happened over the next few years that made me reexamine what this was. I always felt connected with the families I worked with as a speech pathologist. I never crossed a professional relationship with a personal one.

There are times when I meet people and I just have a connection. I met this family while doing speech therapy. While I was there, the mother and I began to speak about her daughter and things to practice at home to help her daughter start to use more words. I heard a voice. I had a feeling it was her grandmother. It was not appropriate for me to discuss this during the speech session. I was so at odds with this. It felt so unprofessional to discuss this with a parent. I didn't know what to do but it kept happening while I was there. So, after tossing it around in my mind I called her and shared and asked how she felt about mediums and intuitive people. She shared she loves watching those shows and she has gone to many on her own. I could feel her excitement. Her eyes lit up when she spoke, but her voice was loving as she shared her past experiences with the medium. She felt so lucky to feel her grandmother's presence. She explained how her skin prickles when she feels her presence around her. I decided to tell her that I had received a message and asked her if she was interested to know what I heard. She was so ecstatic. I came to her house three times a week and I usually stayed longer and shared the messages I got. I said *I didn't know how I did what I did.* I was very new at all of this. She was so encouraging me to pursue this. She was the first person outside of my family with whom I shared my intuitive gifts. Her belief in me meant so much to me. The messages had meaning to her. She was so thrilled that her grandma connected through me to her. She had a sense she was around, but she didn't know how to receive information from her. From then on, I would get information whenever I was near her. She adored her and it brought her so much comfort and joy to get any information. Months later I sensed she was pregnant. I had a sense it was going to be a boy. Her grandmother confirmed this and said that he would have personality traits like her dad. I predicted her due date. I found the more I shared with her the more I was able to share information. I shared information I just felt as well. I received information that allowed her to create a thriving business that is still expanding today. It was the first time I was transparent about my gifts.

It meant so much to me that I could convey information to her. I didn't know how I did it, but I knew that the information I channeled for her to communicate to her grandmother was real and she encouraged me to pursue this gift. I knew I needed to.

We are still in touch, and she is gifted and intuitive. It is amazing that I have an opportunity to assist her in her journey to step into her intuitive gifts.

I couldn't just let it simmer on the back burner. I didn't know how! I was curious and eager to learn more. The fear of what I would uncover kept me stuck. I somehow knew once I started this it would shift the foundation of my life. It would alter the way I perceive things. I was so worried about rocking the boat. It was easier to leave things as they were. I was becoming more out of sorts, I couldn't sleep; my stomach was a mess; I had aches in my neck, back of my head, and headaches. I was convinced it was perimenopause. I was emotional and on edge. One evening I was making a cup of tea and I heard my mother-in-law's voice, "It's in the coffee cup."

I heard it several times in a row. I don't know what made me think to go into the basement, but I did. I kept hearing the message, "in the cup white cup." I took my cabinet apart and found underneath a white coffee cup a blackened bracelet. I polished it off. I remembered this bracelet I purchased when my mother-in-law was in her last days. She told me what to get and I went and got this bracelet for my son and a heart pendant for my daughter. They both had the same inscription: "all my love, Grandma." I started to cry. I couldn't believe she had spoken to me. She spoke to me from time to time to tell my husband she loved him in Yiddish. This time was different. I ran upstairs and told my husband the story and showed him the bracelet. His eyes opened wide, and he was speechless. I knew he knew I heard this message and I felt ten feet tall. Validation! My energy was electromagnetic; I was tingly from head to toe. I saw Kevin's face and I knew what happened was real to him. As I am writing this, I remember the feeling in my body so unsure of his response. I knew what I knew but really was seeking outside validation to resonate with my truth. I felt as if he could acknowledge this event, well, then, it was real. It does sound ludicrous now but, at that time I had no idea what was happening, and I had no one to ask.

I was so programmed to wait for approval before I began to trust it for myself. I began to meditate and found it easy to leave my conscious mind. I started going to more yoga events where people dabbled with this sort of thing. Things were shifting in my life; my stepmother was ill with Parkinson's disease and dementia, and my dogs were not doing well. I felt like things were unraveling and I was at a loss at how to hold it all together. I was tired of working so hard. My life as a speech pathologist meant I was running around constantly. I felt like my whole career in speech was to provide services for families. I prided myself in my education, my certifications, skills, and years of experience. But I started to feel like there was more. I had value that came from who I was and knew I needed to explore it.

When my stepmother's illness became worse many of my clients were upset that I was canceling sessions. I understood they wanted what was best for their child. I felt like who I was, and my expertise didn't matter as much as providing the service. In the end I walked around with guilt for not supporting my dad, brother, and sister with my stepmother's illness. I knew I needed to come to terms with my own feelings too. I felt like this was my moment to choose myself. So, I canceled sessions, and realized that I didn't want to go through the motions in therapy. I knew I needed to be present with everything that was happening. I realized that I tied my worth and value up in all the degrees I had. All the certifications I gained over the years. How many clients I saw and how much money I brought in. I loved what I did. It brought me so much joy to work with children and their families on how to communicate. I loved looking at each child and figuring out the puzzle that would create a shift in how they could formulate sounds. I spent hours thinking about vocabulary and crafts to create with them. I loved this work. But

I still felt undervalued inside. There was a piece of me that felt I was missing something big. I enrolled in coaching school, and it was great to be around people who were seeking to explore who they were, and I was fascinated with functional medicine. So I thought I would be a functional health coach. Along the way I discovered as much as I loved functional medicine and holistic health my heart was in helping people to discover their inner worth. So, let me share some coach insight here. Coaches tend to specialize in areas where they themselves are seeking to gain wisdom. I spent most of my life wondering if I was seen, waiting for someone to notice and validate my value and worth. I never understood that it needed to begin with me. I focused on pleasing others and took time to stop and listen but shared little with most people about me. I didn't pursue the one thing that kept showing up in my life because of fear. I always had this inclination to understand things beyond what I learned or read. I could connect with spiritual energy. I never claimed it or explored what I could learn. It was time I wanted to learn more. I made a decision to be open to what comes my way. I was ready to expand.

Juicy Nuggets

When our truth comes knocking on the door it is up to us to open the door. I closed the door so many times to my truth because of fear. If you close your eyes and breathe, let your breath get even and ask what my truth is. Then this is the hard part: be brave enough to listen to the unspoken answer. Many times we know deep inside when things are not as they should be. Having the faith and courage to change the momentum that is in your life allows you to direct your path. I say better to notice when the path feels out of sync than to keep going on a course that is not allowing you to be the truest expression of who you are meant to be. Sometimes that means changing jobs, but it could also mean carving out time to be open to discover what brings you joy.

Create time in your life to explore it. Create the life you dare to dream of instead of dreaming the life you dream of having.

> **AFFIRMATION**
>
> I am the Creator of my life

> **INSPIRATION**
>
> Create a dream

39

THE DIFFERENCE BETWEEN FEAR AND EXCITEMENT IS PERSPECTIVE.

Use that energy; turn it into anticipation. Go, go, go.

I always was able to recognize fear. It settled into my stomach and the energy seeped into my veins and held me in there. It usually came in the midst of indecision. When a part of me wanted to trust my own instincts and the other part doubted my initial self-confidence. There have been many times I have been excited about something and then in the end it did not pan out the way I hoped. I would lose momentum and inspiration. We all have those moments when we feel like we stumbled upon an incredible idea. There are only a few of us who actually pursue it past the initial idea. I used to think it was because those people had a better idea or more creativity. I have learned it is because they were able to move past their fear and use the energy to propel them forward.

I noticed that when I began coaching, I was so unsure how to communicate what I did I found myself offering everything I did. I was impatient. Being in that energy was confusing and frustrating for me. I felt like any step forward was complicated with hours of me second-guessing all my choices. I was living in scarcity. I was so worried about not being enough value, not having enough to offer, that people wouldn't want to work with me. The result was me giving away my time for free. Offering so much to prove my worth. Along the way I learned more about myself but the biggest thing I learned was to forgive myself when things didn't work and to trust myself when I wanted to try things. The biggest one was to tune in to what resonated with me. I showed up every week with my figurative backhoe to move past my fear and find a way to move forward authentically. The truth is it takes a village. We think we need to work harder. The truth is we all do this. So now I have learned the only way to begin something that you believe in is to surround yourself with people who you can count on that have your vision and can be your cheerleader. Being in a space to be an innovator, a creative thinker, a writer, a speaker, and a visionary takes a certain amount of freedom to dream and believe that your vision will improve people's lives. The other part is having the ability to stick with your idea, especially when you feel like it is challenging, keeping you away from change.

CHANNEL

Transform your fear
into unbounding courage.
Away from a dream
Affirmation I surrender to fear it is a teacher
In truth there is a place of freedom
where we can claim time in space
what do you need to know?
acceptance
there is no particular place l where magic exists
it is not a place
it is awareness of what can be
it is the potential of what is possible
Where faith resides
faith is belief
what is the Hope
It is not a definitive feeling
it emerges from doubt
Hope is deceiving; it feels like positive energy
Until you consider
You are holding energy for
Failure

When energy is stagnant
there is no use of power
The power to be more than what you see
In a moment we are challenged to dare to dream
Dream of a reality that is in the future
possibility is
where you are putting your faith and trust
into what you believe
The energy of love is part of that dream
it is a powerful energy that is beyond rationality and explanation
is faith in another
faith in yourself
it is when ego is still in the face of believing what we can hold but only
feel
It is when you have acceptance
for the ideas and notions of what you desire in the future
without it being placed in your hand
to be in a place of love and light and faith
It is seeking light
when you create the space where life dwells
the desires of what you envision for your life
will rain upon you
for the love that you have for yourself
the trust and faith create an energy

AFFIRMATION

Be an innovator

INSPIRATION

Expansion with love

40

SEE YOURSELF IN YOUR EYES, NOT THE EYES OF ANOTHER.

There was a strum of excitement in the air. My teacher, Mrs. Winick, was telling us to put our things away and get our lunch boxes and get in line. I loved lunchtime. It was fun to be independent and eat with my friends. I remember one day I put my napkin out on the table and took my lunch out. I pulled out my grapes, apple juice, and my sandwich. When I opened my sandwich there was only half. I checked in my bag but there was nothing in there except napkins.

I ate what was there and was confused about what had happened to my lunch. When I got home, I told my mom what had happened. She said, "Yes, I gave you half because you're getting fat." I didn't understand what she was talking about. I could tell it wasn't good by the tone of her voice. I felt like I had done something wrong. All I wanted to know was how to fix it. She didn't say much else. I didn't think much about it then but in the years to come I would. It would hurt when she told me to suck in my stomach and chuckle with her friend while looking at pictures and commenting on how I looked pregnant in a picture. When we went shopping, she redirected me to wear a one-piece bathing suit because girls like me didn't wear bikinis. I never said anything, but each comment stung, and it made me feel inadequate. I was always on alert trying to please her and my dad, not sure exactly how I could fix this. I wanted to please them. It was who I was. I would keep my feelings tucked away and just strive to make them happy. I spent so much time while I was young trying to mold myself to be what everyone needed to be. I pretty much believed it was my job to be what my dad, sister, and stepmother wanted. Things just seemed to work better when I was compliant and had no voice. Of course this strategy works when you're four years old. I remember my only goal was to bring some happiness back into my dad's eyes. I don't remember everything clearly, but I do remember his sadness. When I could make him smile and change how he felt I felt so important and valuable. So without even consciously choosing I made it my responsibility to bring him joy when I could. It gave me a sense of purpose and pride. I can see now of course that this wasn't my job. On a subconscious level I feel I have been protecting him from my true feelings to protect him from pain my whole life.

I am a firm believer that the obstacles in life are here for us to gain wisdom. Some lessons take longer than others to process. In this case I have been blaming my stepmother's relationship with food for the reason why I had a bad relationship with food and my body image. The truth is that I was holding onto so many feelings. It was easier for me to focus on my relationship with food than my relationship with my body or the one that didn't exist with my stepmother. I remember always feeling like an outcast, never quite fitting in, I had a different point of view and I always felt misunderstood. When I lived in college, I developed my own rhythm of doing things and didn't think much about food. I began to see myself and really started on a trajectory of self-discovery. I was fortunate that my dad paid for college, and I could use that time to figure out how to dream. I think I always had my family's approval in my mind. I wish I could tell you I let go of the anger, but I didn't do that until much later. I spent so many years looking for approval in everything I did. I began to need it less when I got married. The funny thing was I was still my father's daughter when we would go visit. I would become very anxious and when I gained weight after getting married my dad would comment on it. No matter my accomplishments or how old my children were when I went to my parents' house I was back in that story. The outcast, the one who was misunderstood, I let that story become my identity instead of seeing how much of my power I was giving away. I thought standing in my power meant asking my father to stop making comments about my body size. I didn't realize that I needed to accept and acknowledge all of myself first.

We are handed lessons in our life, and when we are ready, we can see the wisdom.

I continued to look outside of myself for approval. I needed to learn how to acknowledge myself. When I started to see who I was by tapping into my intuitive gifts I was able to find compassion for my dad and stepmother. I know that they truly did the best they could. It is up to me to give myself compassion and acknowledge all of me. I also know that looking for approval and acceptance outside myself was a pattern I could get stuck in. It was easier to seek approval outside of myself because it was what I knew. I never even considered doing it another way, until much later in my life. I had confidence in myself to some degree, but I was burnt by a lot of bullying when I was younger and found myself in many relationships where I simply went along with what most people thought. I somehow never knew what it was like to do things without seeking approval. It dumbfounded me that I even sought it from my husband and kids. I realized that I needed to stop looking outside of myself. I did the work to discover what I was thinking. Stepping into my intuitive gifts allowed me to trust what I know to be true. It allowed me to have faith in myself and begin to listen to what I thought. I began to appreciate my gifts and use them in my work and in my life. This is the kind of work I personally love to do because in the end the people I work with feel a stronger sense of self-awareness and trust about who they are and what they are here to do.

Juicy Nuggets

It is easy to carry around stories from when we are younger and allow them to suspend and almost inhibit your magnificence. We all have the power to have the ability to discover a new level of compassion for ourselves. Forgive yourself for allowing the story to have a strong influence on you. Here is what you need to know: the stronger the influence the bigger the change. When you let go of the judgment you are holding, you get to unearth the wisdom. That wisdom will forever be your ally. Things show up in our lives for a reason and when we have the strength to unravel them, we can discover our authentic soul.

CHANNEL

Hold tight to the belief
the notion that each of us
has the right to discover our true self
we cannot hand it to each other
like you would a treasure stone.
We need to have faith and trust
in them to discover who they are
the inner work needs to be done
to discover what drives us
Is revealed by living day to day
in the mundane activities of life
many of us feel as though
we stumble upon our gifts
having no memory
when the exact moment was when
we discovered our gift
it is gently pet placed within our soul
emerges when we are ready to see it.
Each of us discovering
coveting our gifts as the true treasures they are
It is free will that propels us forward to
Step into who we are with courage

AFFIRMATION

Authentic soul

INSPIRATION

See yourself

41

The Universe Can Provide Just What You Desire Once You Hold onto the Idea that You Are Worthy.

I used to think that validation of who I was came from outside of me. When I was younger, I looked to my parents, my sister, and my brother. Then I looked at my teachers and friends. I spent so much time trying to fit into the mold that others set for me. It wasn't until recently that I realized that:

Living your life to perform for others doesn't allow you to align with your thoughts.

Reflecting your identity based on the way others see you is destructive.

Loving someone doesn't mean you always agree.

Not being authentic only hurts *you*.

I have struggled with the idea that my value is simply me just being me. That I don't need to do more. I remind myself often because it was a hard lesson for me to grasp. I was taught, like most of us, that we are valuable by how well we perform. When I was younger, I learned this from a smile from my family or by seeing them clap their hands. Later on it was gold stars on my schoolwork. It seemed like I was always waiting for some outside source to tell me just how well I was doing. Until I got to high school and felt that things weren't so cut and dry. During college and even grad school, grades indicated how worthy I was. Then later the gold stars vanished, and I was left to decide for myself if I was doing well. This was a scary proposition and I remember feeling finally I can decide my direction. I could trust my own instincts. I had done it before. Somehow, I became disconnected from what I knew. I was seeking outside direction feeling inadequate, and at the same time resenting when someone implied I didn't know something. I was angry at the need to ask and scared to trust myself to know for sure. I never felt like I knew what to do. I was always asking people's opinions. I remember asking so many people I ended up even more confused. I very seldom voiced my opinion about what to do with my friends and was eager to participate to be a part of the group. What I couldn't see was that by not allowing my ideas to have a voice I was saying that those ideas had no merit. It felt like inside of me I had strong ideas, but rarely did I ever stand my ground. I instead complained and felt as though I was unseen, unheard and undervalued. Once I started to understand that my voice and wisdom mattered, I started to feel more comfortable wearing those "big girl" pants. It was something I slipped on and slipped off. Trying it on over and over until it actually felt more authentic to use my voice to claim who I was than to sit back and not share my own ideas. If you met me five years ago you wouldn't say I was a pushover. I had a big personality. I was using my energy in a way that didn't serve me. I was leaking energy everywhere. Getting overwhelmed by taking on tasks that I didn't know how to say no to. I had issues with creating boundaries. I didn't know how to budget my time. I was late everywhere. I felt I had to do it all. I never considered how to say no. I didn't know my worth separate from my actions. I was what others wanted me to be. I thought being needed showed my worth and value. I didn't know what I wanted. I wasn't sure what defined me. So when I stopped asking and started listening to myself, I was able to uncover my authentic self. That was the real work, discovering who I was, accepting my gifts, and claiming them as mine.

Juicy Nuggets

Let me share a Robinism in other words things I say over and over based on my own flavor of wisdom. From the moment we are born we are sponges. We learn how to create different crying patterns to get picked up and fed. We learn that our parents smile, and eye contact can let us know if we are doing a good job or if they are disappointed. Then we shape our behaviors to continue to get that positive feedback. This is what most children do with some exceptions. As we grow, we begin to look at our teachers, coaches, and other significant people in our lives for acknowledgments of our physical and theoretical gold star that we are doing well. As we go to college the positive feedback diminishes and we begin to rely more on what we think. This prepares us for our careers where we use our own sense of conscience to guide our work ethic. This is how we develop a reputation based on our skills. Our rewards come when we get a bonus or are asked to take on a challenging project.

I started to think about this. I released that we are still ultimately waiting for approval that comes outside of ourselves. So many of us take on more than we should to prove how capable we are. Continuing to seek that gold star.

Here is what I didn't know: by doing it all I was always looking for validation like a gold star. "Good job!" I felt like I was forever waiting to be acknowledged and appreciated. I was so focused on the appreciation. I was still looking outside of me to feel like I was valuable. I did have moments where I would feel a sense of accomplishment on my own. I couldn't see that by doing it all I was not allowing other people in my family to step up and do what they could. I was not valuable because I cooked or ran an errand and sure it was appreciated but it didn't allow me to fully express who I was and what I needed inside. There was no number of manicures or massages that could fix that. I had to uncover myself.

CHANNEL

The spirit of friendship in acceptance of you
is not a place for bartering
Can acceptance of self be a commodity
Can it be something you trade
How much sacrifice does one need to take on
Before the realization
acceptance has no price

The story you tell yourself
how you allow more into your life
The truth is all is there
for you to hold
once you allow it to know
You are worth it

AFFIRMATION

I accept myself

INSPIRATION

Connecting to your guides

42

HAVING TRUST IN YOURSELF
TAKES PRACTICE.

It sort of just happened when I started to think about the idea that I was having a baby. I started nesting almost instantly. I started planning all the things that I wanted to have for this new baby. What I wanted his room to look like. How I wanted the house to look. I started to imagine how it was all going to unfold. I had this notion in my head about how perfect it was all going to be. After all, I told myself, I am a speech pathologist. I worked with babies. I was an expert. I knew what to expect. What could go wrong, right? Here's what I didn't know. Any plan that you have when you're pregnant goes completely out the window when you can't sleep. The excitement of rushing to the hospital and having everyone visit catches up especially when you are woken up every forty-five minutes to nurse. Kevin and I would work together but we were exhausted. So my body desperately wanted to rest. My whole body ached. Kevin and I worked together but Jason was difficult to comfort. All I knew was I had a baby that kept on crying. I would walk with him, rock with him, nurse him and nothing soothed him. Just when I thought things were getting better and he was eating with more efficiency he would projectile vomit all over me and I would start to worry and wonder about what a crappy mother I was. How was he going to gain weight? I was alone a lot, and my husband went back to work. It was freezing outside so going out was out of the question. My brain was screaming at me that it wanted stimulation, conversation, laughter, a good book maybe. I could not find the energy to do anything. I didn't expect this. Who was I becoming?

During this time my mother-in-law would take a train and walk to my house to do my son's laundry. She came several times a week. She always brought food and she just listened. One day she came in. I was still wearing my housecoat crying after cleaning up another mess of my son throwing up all over me. She looked at me and smiled and said, "Go take a shower. Let me hold him; go take care of yourself." It was like gold, as if somebody had given me the most ideal gift in the entire world to take care of myself. The next few moments that were utter bliss involved me taking a shower and simply not worrying If I was right or if I was wrong. I was able to gather myself together so I could try again. I realized something: all the worrying had energy. I was transferring this energy to my son while he was nursing. It hit me while I was drying my hair. It made so much sense. Of course he could feel my energy and my trepidation. Children are so perceptive they can tell when someone is unsure or eager. I knew I had figured out something huge and it would change how I was feeling. I felt empowered that I could change this situation. Before I could nurse him again, I came up with a plan. I would hold him close to me and close my eyes. Imagine that I was giving him all of my love in energy. I imagined that he was going to stay calm and be calm all through the nursing and that the more he drank the calmer he would become. He would grow and flourish. I stopped judging myself as a failure and developed more insight and patience. This was not the first time I thought of planning the outcome and then working backward toward my goal. It made sense to me to identify what I desired and then create the energy needed with my actions and thoughts to allow it to unfold as I wanted. I didn't realize until many years later that I was trusting my intuition to get through this difficult time. I didn't know what it was called. I didn't even know why I thought of it or how. I knew this was what I needed to do. It worked! The funny thing is when push comes to shove while I was in my younger years, and I needed to make a decision because of an emergency situation or because it was crucial for me to make a decision, I just made one. I wondered why I couldn't make decisions about smaller things. Why did I struggle with what to make for dinner, what shirt to wear to a party, what shoes to pair with my shirt? The things that were pretty insignificant would give me a lot of anxiety. I never seem to be able to make a clear-cut decision efficiently. I was always wondering about the judgment of others. It seemed that when there was an urgent situation it was easier to make choices. Maybe it's because there is no room to second guess yourself. In an emergency there is no time to ponder all the choices or what someone else might do. I just needed to act. Trust my intuition. When you're in an urgent situation, that situation allows you to trust your first instinct because there's no time to second guess yourself. My intuition and the girth of my intuition was learning to trust myself: period. This is why I know we all have intuition, and it's our choice to do more with it. Funny thing is when I think about those emergencies and the choices I made, they were spot on. I believe we all have untapped magic called intuition. When we are in circumstances that require quick decision-making, we make a choice. We use our intuition to guide us to the decisions we need to make. Those decisions are automatic and usually spot-on. It is when we overthink our gut decisions. We move away from our intuition and instead move into the land of logical thinking. Logical thinking has its place. I believe that if we want to develop our intuitive side, we need to dwell in the space of instinct. That is where we can discover trust in who we are and develop a relationship with who we are. Then we can start to appreciate our intrinsic value.

SOMETHING TO CONSIDER

The truth is if I had trusted myself long ago, making decisions would have been a lot less stressful. When situations were not emergent my ego would chime in and stir up doubt. Ego is a funny thing. We get it confused with our intuition. The difference is our ego will have us feeling less than. Our intuition will empower our choices.

CHANNEL

Rebellion is a state the ego is in to protect the idea that giving up
Power of self is extinguishing your voice— self and wisdom
What if you could honor it, value it, then your ego can be hushed
Only to
Show when newness is upon us to create doubt of your innate worth
Raise your frequency high and allow your ego to
Feel
Love and compassion like you would
A child
Then know that is not your reality any longer.
You have learned a new story
Your ego has Peter Pan syndrome and is stuck in what was
Where doubt lives
Where lack lives
Where uncertainty lives
Move over ego
Create the space of possible
Where love lives
Where abundance lives

AFFIRMATION

Solutions will come to me
with ease and grace

INSPIRATION

Let the light heal your soul

43

Gratitude Is Believing Goodness Is Coming and Being Open to Receive It and Grateful When It Arrives.

This may sound controversial, but I am not in alignment with the new trend of keeping a gratitude journal. Let me explain why; *gratitude* is a state of being a feeling you have. Gratitude journals have become a way for people to list what they have in their life and take the time to see it and appreciate what they have. Inner gratitude is about feeling a sense of connection and appreciation for who you are. In order to receive gratitude you need to know inside that you have deep worth and value. So it is a feeling that you develop from the inside and when you have a sense of knowing who you are you discover a new state of awareness, confidence, and trust in yourself. That is how we can learn to trust ourselves to make decisions with confidence. We learn to quiet all the voices inside of ourselves that seem to be screaming when we begin to take the scary steps to believe. Let your inner critic go if you stop to listen you could be squandering your dreams. If we open and surrender to the idea that possibility is not just for a movie star or your next-door neighbor. We need to consider that possibility is available to anyone who is willing to receive the spark of ingenuity. Did you ever notice when there are new movie trailers being released, they sound the same? There are many people who get the spark of information but not everyone will trust in their ability to execute and create something with it. The reason shark tank is such a hit is that everyone knows that the spark can touch anyone who is tuning in. It is what we do with it. Do we let our ego talk us out of it? Do we take a chance and trust that this idea is in alignment with what lights us up?

In order for me to do more than dream, I needed to start by believing I deserved my dream to come true. I had to do the work to believe I had value, worth, fortitude, intelligence, and compassion to be able to see it come true. In order to write this book I needed to unearth all of these things and let go of the notion that I couldn't receive the prize, which for me is this book. Now is the time for me to bestow the same love, compassion, patience, and insight I give everyone I care about and shine the light back onto myself.

No matter how far I think I have grown personally I still find that I seek validation. I am the kind of person who likes to share ideas. Then it dawned on me recently, that when I am quiet and *"puttering"* about I get the best information. It isn't like I get streams of thoughts all the time but while I am moving sound quietly, I am processing all the messages I have gotten—no matter how far I think I have grown personally I sometimes still seek validation outside of myself. I am the kind of person who likes to share ideas. Then it dawned on me recently, that when I am quiet and *"puttering"* about I get the best information. It isn't like I get streams of thoughts all the time but while I am moving sound quietly, I am processing all the messages I have gotten. I am abundant and grateful.

Juicy Nuggets

It is much easier to give and much harder to receive. To receive you need to first believe you are worthy.

You've had wisdom all along. Go within to seek the answers and believe that you have the wisdom of many. When we ask for validation outside it is because we believe our own answers are not enough. Seeking support from another does not mean getting the answers but being supported to discover them.

Daily practices I use:

Flip your judgments into wisdom and find your own path.

Look at judgment as wisdom.

I am thoughtful when I speak to myself.

If you want others to see wisdom in you, you need to witness it for yourself.

Find the courage to speak your truth especially when your voice shakes.

Remember that speaking your truth is a birthright—no voice is too small to be heard.

Put a voice behind the thoughts your soul recognizes as truth.

Be the person you can count on to make yourself feel cherished and loved.

Allowing myself to receive satisfaction, value, and worth does not just come when we serve but it comes when we allow ourselves to receive.

Love comes from within; it shines bright and attracts those who have discovered the same.

Seek what you want from the world, inside you.

CHANNEL

Speak to the world the way you want to be spoken to.
How can we speak to others in a way that is
not what we desire for ourselves?
No voice is too small to be heard.
There is no such thing as a small voice.
Every voice has enough energy and light to be heard.
Love yourself life takes on new colors sounds
simple but it is about declaring to ourselves what we choose
create a practice.
Love all your parts

especially the imperfect ones
Those imperfect parts
allow discovering our compassion
for ourselves

AFFIRMATION

My wisdom lights me up

INSPIRATION

Nurture the dream

44

DAYDREAMING IS FOR WARRIORS.

We all have dreams that we manifest into reality. Thinking and daydreaming are key to being a creative person. In order to manifest your dream you need faith.

How do you start to have faith? Well, you need to lean into your intuition. When you start to trust your intuitive side, you begin to see that you can believe in what is not physical. I heard other people would see images and receive signs. I was impatient and learning all of this. It was challenging to believe and trust myself. This was a hard thing for me at the beginning to grasp. So I started to ask my guides to show me in ways I understand that I am on the right track. I saw a rainbow in my house, a praying mantis, and a peacock showed up at my door. Each time I saw something magical I texted my mentor. I wasn't ready to trust my own intuitive meaning. I was still seeking acknowledgments outside of myself looking to someone I believed had more wisdom than me.

My mentor gifted me a deck of tarot cards. She laid out several decks and told me to pick one. I remember looking at them all and one became illuminated, and I knew it was the one I connected to. She suggested that I pull cards and see what each card meant to me. There was no book, nor did I think to look online. I knew I needed to connect intuitively and discover the meaning through my connection. The deck sat on my night table. I took it out of its' velvet satchel from time to time, but I felt so much information that I could break it down. Well, that was the story I told myself. It was too hard; I wasn't able to do this. I reached my limit in my spiritual growth blah, blah, blah. I had sessions with her she never asked me how it was going, and I felt that I got away without confronting my block. Wrong! Several weeks later, I had a session with her, and she asked me how it was going. I told her the whole sad story. She simply said, "Do you have the cards?" I confessed I did, using my small voice which is very unlike me. I just felt defeated. She said, "Pull three cards and read them for me." After my brain exploded I did just that. I couldn't believe how easy it was. How the information flowed and how I just was able to understand it. That was my first time reading cards. I shared this story with a good friend, and I decided to bring them to a retreat. I remember packing them in my carry-on luggage and then putting them in my pocketbook out of some unrealistic fear that my carry-on luggage would be lost. I was nervous the whole time because I knew this would change things. It was another way for me to share who I was. I offered to pull cards for free just to play around with this new skill. My friend sat next to me the whole time. I pulled cards for a few people. I was a flurry of energy, and I began to understand that I was reading their energy. The card readings were a way for me to connect. I felt like it allowed me a clear path to have insight for them and each time the card resonated I felt ten feet tall. I was doing it! At the same time I was worried that people thought I was a carnival trick. I felt like a tarot reader I saw at carnivals with the hourglass. I had more work to do to accept this gift as a way for me to connect. To claim my gift as a part of me and trust it. I worked on letting go of my judgment of how people use their gifts. That truth triggered me because I wanted to fully embrace all of myself. I wanted to scream. It seemed like every step toward acceptance was met with resistance by me. I eventually saw that all of us get to use our skills in a way that resonates with us. Which is amazing since I believe that we are searching for a person that resonates with us. We get to have that choice.

Juicy Nuggets

I was so nervous I could do it fundamentally. Our worth is recognizing our light and compassion for all we are. I just began to pull cards for my friends on the phone and each time they would respond with positive feedback which encouraged me to do more. At the same time I was exploring this new gift I was feeling mixed emotions because I knew that what I wanted to do was more than reading cards. I was on a mission to work with people to trust their intuition. I knew we all had intuition and that when we trust it, our lives have more abundance because we live in the abundance of who we are and don't know how to share this. I felt that oracle card reading was a skill. Eventually I could just see a name and pick up on their energy. This skill was a door opener for me to trust my skills and know that oracle cards are a way for me to get specific information. This communicates how much the universe has to offer when I open my heart to receive the information. To trust that the information I need is there. The card provides tangible proof of the energy I am reading and provides an anchor for the person to see and witness.

Channel

Daydreaming is for Warriors
Let go; let go of the ideas
that have knitted into your mind
that have allowed you to craft a story
about who you actually are
Do they come from someone else's perspective
another set of eyes
another viewpoint
another story
if you were to let them go
who would you be
could you craft a new story

Of who you are
without those eyes
of another looking on
you could be anything
Let it take shape
in your mind
you can be
what you dream
could you allow
your mind to meander
into all the things
that you could be
all the things that you
can't even see
with clarity
Things you can only sense
Let go of the judgments
They hold us back
from the allowing our minds want to expand
consider all that we can be
Those judgments were not meant
To hold us back
they were meant to be a guide
even a spotlight
to see where we need to expand
When we were young
they were meant to keep us safe
our young minds misread them
misunderstood those ideas
the people who looked upon us
gave us rules
how they believed we needed to live our lives
what if they were merely suggestions
to keep us safe in the moment

we are not those little ones anymore
we are in a new place on a new timeline
we get to craft the stories
that we want to dream
That we want to live
To live our daydream

AFFIRMATION

I am able live my daydream

INSPIRATION

Manifest your dreams

45

ASK THE UNIVERSE FOR THE SUPPORT YOU NEED AND HAVE FAITH.

Sometimes I can't tell the difference between a daydream and an idea. A daydream for me it's a thought that's in the future that I would like to see happen. An idea is a vision of something that I would like to do but I haven't quite figured out how it will unfold. These visions used to scare me because I was stuck in the notion of how I was going to make them happen. I've since learned that one passion is the underlying cause for my ideas and that with time, I can create them. I really think that everyone can do this but what stops us is this underlying fear that we are not capable enough. We all get stuck in all the pieces that it might take and the success rate and how good or bad this idea will take route. What if you could take it all off the table? What if you create ideas and make them happen and simply look at their outcomes as information and analyze this information and see what you learned. Now this philosophy is not one that came to me easily; it was something that my coaches and mentors taught me. I wish I could say that I swallow the failures with dignity and grace each time but that would be a lie. The truth is failure is sometimes hard and takes me longer to recover from. Now I've learned that they are like seeds you plant in the garden, some take and some just don't. It's nothing personal. You put it out there, that's the hard part and then you see where this idea goes. This kind of attitude has allowed me to create new things over and over again and I probably will continue to do this with many of them not evolving the way I thought that they would. I love creating new ideas and seeing how they work out. This used to be something I was scared of but now with this new understanding that I'm just planting seeds it's allowed me to let go of the outcome.

CHANNEL

RECEIVE

Look beyond what's right in front of you
see beyond what's your eyes can see
if you were allowing your eyes
Could see what's unseen
energy would become clear.
You can try and think through your problems
you can try to read them all
the truth is when you use intuition trust
what's your wisdom already knows
the problems that appear
magically become clear
things that seem like they have no answers
have solutions
When we look with our eyes
We forget to trust what we know
the information we need
Comes to us
it appears
Be open to noticing it
having faith in what you cannot see
having trust in who you are
Having the ability to see that you are supported
being able to see without your eyes
be able to trust in

what is coming your way
It is all a gift from the universe
Open your heart
Receive it
Drink it in

AFFIRMATION

I see all of me

INSPIRATION

First trust yourself

AFTERWORD

I was on my way to a retreat. I was really looking forward to spending time with a close friend of mine and connecting to so many more. Meanwhile, my mind kept recalling a friend named Sara whom I had met at retreats along the way. I had a connection to her, and I was interested in exploring how to work with her as a coach. I wanted to grab a moment and see if she was interested in coaching me. I remember sitting down with her outside in a shady spot. We both took our sunglasses off so we could have a heart chat. As soon as we did, I got goosebumps. There was so much energy between us. I felt like she knew what I was talking about before I even said it. I talked about my dreams and how I wanted to work with her to create the momentum to begin to manifest them. We began to coach weekly. I could feel there was a shift coming within me. It feels like a stirring of ideas that are beginning to swirl and take shape. In the beginning I didn't have a clear understanding. I have learned during this time to surrender to the uncertainty and trust that all will be clear. I find myself getting frustrated with the feeling of walking in a haze so to speak, it is hard to focus on creating new ideas or executing new projects. I find myself puttering a lot into creating space to meander and allow information to come to me. I had a sense I was getting closer to a new level of understanding. One day after breakfast I sat down at the computer after breakfast in my PJs and a hot cup of coffee. I opened a new PowerPoint file and began to type. The words just poured out and I channeled the information. As I began to finish the last slide in the PowerPoint I reached for my coffee and noticed it was ice cold. The oat milk on the top had a film over it. I glanced up at the time on my computer and calculated that approximately four hours had gone by. I looked at the PowerPoint on my screen and I noticed the last slide was numbered forty-two. How could that be? I thought I couldn't believe it. I began to read back the slides and I was so ecstatic I realized that these channeled messages were the book. I was meant to share this wisdom. I texted Sara who responded with every emoji that there is. I was buzzing. I sent her a copy of the PowerPoint. In our next coaching session she was thrilled for me but proposed that there may be more suggested that there is a story behind these channeled messages. That was how I began to write this book. Thinking that each essay would provide nuggets of wisdom. That the reader could pick what they needed inspiration from that moment and read that essay. In the meantime Sara started Thought Leader Academy and of course I joined. I was able to meet amazing people who had so much to teach me with their tenacity and courage. After three years of writing on and off this book is the result of my continuing on this journey. What wound up happening is more than I could have imagined. I discovered that as I unearthed all my stories that they began to knit these essays into a book. They began to build on each other and this writing process allowed me to take notice that I am a storyteller, and I am a writer. A stirring voice leaves you unbalanced and disconnected. The truth is very connected. The connection isn't crisp at that moment. I have to trust and surrender the control and just that what is coming in is what I need.

Somewhere in the sharing of these stories I also could see the growth in me. No one is more surprised than me that this project unearthed this all. I realized how fearful I was to share all the parts of myself. Personal thanks to my guy Kevin who supported this whirlwind with love. Special thanks to my kids who kept listening to share. My editor Audrey has taught me to trust the story I want to share. There is no such thing as too much information. The closer I got to the end the more fear would stifle my writing. I joined many joint writing sessions with my friends and my talented friends. One day when I was in my head, my coach Kaela shared this nugget: "You are the channel for the story, and it is yours to share. If not, you then who?" I think it is easy to think that someone else has told this story. I know deep down they haven't because it is my story. I have learned from my mentor Sara. That no one else can tell your story and my story is meant to be shared. So, I dig deep to find the warrior in me to offer this story to those who are meant to read it as a source of comfort, inspiration, and wisdom. That last word still has me hesitating. Even though I pride myself on the deep work I do in one-on-one coaching and small groups. I can see shifts in people all the time as they begin to trust themselves. I still am in awe of the information I receive. I trust it all now.

LIST OF INSPIRATIONS

ABOUT THE AUTHOR

Ever since Robin can remember her dad called her Sunshine, as if he could sense, from the moment of her birth, the energy and light that seemed to surround her. From day one she was always eager to be around people which quickly developed into a passion for talking to people as soon as she was able to speak. This natural delight in deep conversation and desire to be truly present with the people around her resulted in a firm belief that "no voice is too small to be heard." While her innate ability to listen deeply first manifested in a career in speech pathology, it eventually became clear to her that she was spiritually intuitive. There were so many signs of her gift over the years that she consistently squashed, until her own motto, "no voice is too small to be heard," suddenly seemed to apply to her own voice and her own experience. Finally, she was ready to listen to her inner voice, her intuition, and her remarkable ability to channel. She now uses these gifts practicing as an intuitive life coach. The wisdom she has gained from her journey to fully accept the magic of her gift is contained in her debut book, *Trust Your Intuition*.

Robin was born in the Bronx and has lived in New York City her whole life. She loves knowing she can go to shows whenever she wants. She met her husband in college and they definitely grew up together. They have two children, and have had two cats, four dogs and a handful of fish over the past 38 years. You can find out more about Robin and her work at www.robinspollak.com. Robin believes everyone has a purpose and deserves to experience their inherent gifts. She looks forward to helping you discover and live your dreams.

ACKNOWLEDGEMENTS

Kevin, lucky me. I have you at my side. Thanks for getting all the take-out and walking Cooper too many times.

And to my kids, for listening to me speak about this adventure too many times.

And to all my friends (you know who you are) who listened, cried laughed and celebrated me.

To my higher self, thank you for sharing the wisdom.

CPSIA information can be obtained
at www.ICGtesting.com
Printed in the USA
LVHW112144210223
740117LV00019B/403

9 781958 714096